T0021775

The History of Emotions: A Very Short Introduction

VERY SHORT INTRODUCTIONS are for anyone wanting a stimulating and accessible way into a new subject. They are written by experts, and have been translated into more than 45 different languages.

The series began in 1995, and now covers a wide variety of topics in every discipline. The VSI library currently contains over 700 volumes—a Very Short Introduction to everything from Psychology and Philosophy of Science to American History and Relativity—and continues to grow in every subject area.

Very Short Introductions available now:

ABOLITIONISM Richard S. Newman
THE ABRAHAMIC RELIGIONS
    Charles L. Cohen
ACCOUNTING Christopher Nobes
ADDICTION Keith Humphreys
ADOLESCENCE Peter K. Smith
THEODOR W. ADORNO
    Andrew Bowie
ADVERTISING Winston Fletcher
AERIAL WARFARE Frank Ledwidge
AESTHETICS Bence Nanay
AFRICAN AMERICAN HISTORY
    Jonathan Scott Holloway
AFRICAN AMERICAN RELIGION
    Eddie S. Glaude Jr
AFRICAN HISTORY John Parker and
    Richard Rathbone
AFRICAN POLITICS Ian Taylor
AFRICAN RELIGIONS
    Jacob K. Olupona
AGEING Nancy A. Pachana
AGNOSTICISM Robin Le Poidevin
AGRICULTURE Paul Brassley and
    Richard Soffe
ALEXANDER THE GREAT
    Hugh Bowden
ALGEBRA Peter M. Higgins
AMERICAN BUSINESS HISTORY
    Walter A. Friedman
AMERICAN CULTURAL HISTORY
    Eric Avila
AMERICAN FOREIGN RELATIONS
    Andrew Preston
AMERICAN HISTORY Paul S. Boyer

AMERICAN IMMIGRATION
    David A. Gerber
AMERICAN INTELLECTUAL
    HISTORY
    Jennifer Ratner-Rosenhagen
THE AMERICAN JUDICIAL
    SYSTEM Charles L. Zelden
AMERICAN LEGAL HISTORY
    G. Edward White
AMERICAN MILITARY HISTORY
    Joseph T. Glatthaar
AMERICAN NAVAL HISTORY
    Craig L. Symonds
AMERICAN POETRY David Caplan
AMERICAN POLITICAL HISTORY
    Donald Critchlow
AMERICAN POLITICAL PARTIES
    AND ELECTIONS L. Sandy Maisel
AMERICAN POLITICS
    Richard M. Valelly
THE AMERICAN PRESIDENCY
    Charles O. Jones
THE AMERICAN REVOLUTION
    Robert J. Allison
AMERICAN SLAVERY
    Heather Andrea Williams
THE AMERICAN SOUTH
    Charles Reagan Wilson
THE AMERICAN WEST
    Stephen Aron
AMERICAN WOMEN'S HISTORY
    Susan Ware
AMPHIBIANS T. S. Kemp
ANAESTHESIA Aidan O'Donnell

For more information visit our website

www.oup.com/vsi/

Thomas Dixon

THE HISTORY
OF EMOTIONS

A Very Short Introduction

OXFORD
UNIVERSITY PRESS

Great Clarendon Street, Oxford, OX2 6DP,
United Kingdom

Oxford University Press is a department of the University of Oxford.
It furthers the University's objective of excellence in research, scholarship,
and education by publishing worldwide. Oxford is a registered trade mark of
Oxford University Press in the UK and in certain other countries

Published in the United States of America by Oxford University Press
198 Madison Avenue, New York, NY 10016, United States of America

British Library Cataloguing in Publication Data

Data available

Library of Congress Control Number: 2023930639

ISBN 978-0-19-881829-8

Printed and bound by
CPI Group (UK) Ltd, Croydon, CR0 4YY

For Laurie Dixon

Contents

Preface

It is a great pleasure to be able to share my experience of researching and teaching the history of emotions over many years with a new generation of students and readers through this book. I hope it will convey some of my enthusiasm for this subject, as a way both to enrich our understanding of the past and to liberate and inspire us in the present.

There is no view from nowhere, and this *Very Short Introduction* reflects my own position in the world and my preoccupations as a historian. As in the history of emotions as a whole, this book takes many of its examples from western history, and often traces key ideas back to classical, Christian, or Renaissance sources. The book perhaps reflects my own interests in other ways too, for instance by focusing on questions of language and terminology, and on the moral and medical dimensions of feeling.

Nonetheless, I have written the book in a way that is intended to invite others in. I have looked for opportunities to include examples from outside the worlds of Europe and North America, and to make comparisons between western and non-western ideas about feelings and emotions.

I hope that readers will experience this book as an opportunity to think afresh about their emotions—and their history—and as an inspiration to take the ideas and methods of the history of emotions and apply them to newer and wider fields.

Acknowledgements

It is about 25 years since I started thinking about the history of emotions. That was during my time as a Ph.D. student, when I was trying to figure out the difference between 'the passions of the soul' and 'the emotions' in medieval and modern texts. At that time, at the Faculty of Divinity in Cambridge, Fraser Watts, John Milbank, and others encouraged me to think more historically about 'the emotions', in the context of what had started out as a more purely theoretical thesis on theological and secular ideas about feelings.

In more recent years, at the Queen Mary Centre for the History of the Emotions, I have had the opportunity to focus on the subject in a sustained way, supported by many brilliant colleagues. The Centre was founded at the suggestion of Colin Jones, and it has been a successful team endeavour from the outset, drawing on the expertise and energy of many individuals since 2008, including Fay Bound Alberti, Elena Carrera, Rhodri Hayward, Miri Rubin, Tiffany Watt Smith, Emma Sutton, Jules Evans, Sarah Chaney, Richard Firth-Godbehere, Edgar Gerrard Hughes, Helen Stark, Natalie Steed, Craig Baxter, Agnes Arnold-Forster, Alison Moulds, Anna Boneham, and Ollie Brown.

This *Very Short Introduction* has benefited especially from my experience teaching an undergraduate course on the history of emotions at Queen Mary since 2017. I am grateful to all the students on that course whose research, writing, and questioning have helped me explore and develop my understanding of the subject. Evelien Lemmens and Jenny Pistella co-taught the module with me, and I am very grateful to them for improving the course and enriching it with their own approaches to the topic.

In recent years I have spent some time enjoying the often-emotional world of academic Twitter. As well as getting a feel for the affective dimensions of social media—itself a kind of research, I always tell myself—I have often been able to ask for guidance from fellow emotions scholars and had cause to feel thankful to the many people who replied. Similarly I have learned from the questions and discussions I have taken part in after giving talks about various aspects of my work.

When it came to producing the final text of this book, I was inspired and supported by the work of pioneers in the field of the history of emotions, several of whom I mention below. As co-editor, with Ute Frevert, of the 'Emotions in History' book series at Oxford University Press, I have been in the privileged position of seeing many outstanding histories of emotions through to publication. I have also learned much from those who have taken the history of emotions to new generations of students through their research and writing. There are many such scholars, but I would like especially to pay tribute to Katie Barclay and Rob Boddice, who are both brilliant and reliable guides to the newest work in the field, and whose work I have often turned to in writing this book.

For advice on particular topics, I am grateful to John Lincoln, Michelle Shiota, Kerstin Pahl, Angela Platt, Hayley Kavanagh, Susan Matt, Liesbeth Corens, George Boys-Stones, Sarah Rose Cavanagh, Catherine Rose, Nancy Khalek, Ed Brooker, Maria Awan, Michaela Kalcher, Gail Marshall, Suzy Lawrence, and Imke Rajamani.

I owe a special debt of gratitude to Jo Cohen, Erin Sullivan, Cathleen Mair, and Argyris Stringaris, all of whom were kind enough to comment on draft chapters, and especially to my wife, Emily Butterworth, who read and commented on the whole thing, with her usual combination of perspicuity and tact. At Oxford University Press, Latha Menon provided detailed and much valued feedback on the text, while Karen Hunter worked hard to ensure the best possible versions of images were available as illustrations, and all aspects of production were expertly overseen by Imogene Haslam. My literary agent Anna Power provided encouragement and motivation as always.

This book is dedicated to my brilliant son Laurie. Between us, he and I have pretty much all the emotions covered.

Acknowledgements

List of illustrations

Chapter 1
The pulse of the past

It is hard to think of any significant aspect of the past that did not involve emotions. Everyday life has always been an arena of feeling, within which friendships, feuds, and family dramas are played out. On the political stage, momentous decisions have been motivated by nationalist passions, historic resentments, and sentiments of sympathy and humanity. War, disease, and disaster have been occasions for courage, terror, anguish, and despair. Through the centuries, preachers and agitators have drawn on the enthusiasms and resentments of the people. Composers, artists, and writers have used the power of their imaginations to conjure up whole new worlds of feeling, and even to invent new emotions. Whether we turn our ears to the cries of the oppressed or to the rallying calls of fired-up visionaries, we hear not just the tales of events long past, but the echoes of ancestral emotions. The beat of history is kept by the pulse of the human heart.

Historians have long been aware that their craft is a matter of feeling as well as thinking and, although literary styles have varied widely across the centuries, there is nothing new about using emotions to help bring the past back to life. Narrative histories routinely speculate about the motivations of protagonists, and attribute key decisions to emotional states from jealousy, enmity, or vengeance to devotion, desire, and empathy. The personal loves and losses, joys and griefs of important figures are used to add colour to historical accounts. Like all writers, historians think about the impact of their words on readers, and sometimes represent the lives and thoughts of the past in a way that is designed to move people emotionally in the present. This kind of emotional history reached a particular level of intensity in the works of romantically inclined authors in the 19th century, and especially in debates among historians who had very different feelings about the French Revolution. This disagreement is a good place to start our introduction to the relationship between history and feelings, and to the story of how the history of emotions emerged as a discipline.

What is this thing called *La Révolution*?

In 1837, the Scottish writer Thomas Carlyle produced a three-volume history of the French Revolution. In Carlyle's hands this was a tale of drama, passions, and bloodshed. It read more like a novel than a historical chronicle, with the main characters brought to life as creatures of visceral feeling. Carlyle introduced Maximilien Robespierre, the instigator of the Great Terror, the bloodiest period of the revolution, to his readers in the following terms:

> that anxious, slight, ineffectual-looking man, under thirty, in spectacles; his eyes (were the glasses off) troubled, careful; with upturned face, snuffing dimly the uncertain future-time; complexion of a multiplex atrabiliar colour, the final shade of which may be the pale sea-green.

It was characteristic of Carlyle to use a term that was incredibly obscure even at the time—'atrabiliar', meaning affected by black bile or melancholy. Carlyle's vivid literary style allowed his readers to sense his protagonists as embodied, emotional human beings—almost to see their troubled eyes, catch the tremor in their breath, and to hear their hearts pounding.

2

Carlyle did more, however, than populating his history with flesh-and-blood characters described in the style of a gothic melodrama. He also turned to the appetites and instincts of humanity to try to offer a deeper philosophical explanation of the events he was narrating. Towards the end of his history, looking back at the tumult and the body-count, Carlyle paused to ask himself and his readers a question: 'What, then, is this Thing called *La R é volution* which, like an Angel of Death, hangs over France?' He attempted an answer:

> *La Révolution* is but so many Alphabetic Letters; a thing nowhere to be laid hands on, to be clapt under lock and key: where is it? what is it? It is the Madness that dwells in the hearts of men. In this man it is, and in that man; as a rage or as a terror, it is in all men.

This passage hints at some of the most interesting challenges facing the historian of emotions. For the most part, historians encounter the passions and feelings of the past in the form of words. These might be words written in the heat of passion in a love letter, words printed in a medical treatise about diseases of the mind, words published in a newspaper report of a sensational trial, or words in the lyrics of a song. But very often what the historian of emotions starts with is indeed 'but so many Alphabetic Letters'. Emotions can seem as if they are nowhere to be laid hands on, even when they have left their traces in documents, treasured objects, or physical spaces. Careful, historically informed reading of the visible outward signs of inward and invisible feelings is the central work of historians of emotions. When they encounter words and images, signs that point towards an imagined, invisible thing—a passion, a feeling, an emotion—they ask of that entity, 'What is it? Where is it?'

The second part of Carlyle's answer to his own question sets the scene for further big questions in the history of emotions. He traced the violence and chaos of the French Revolution to the rage, terror, and madness that 'dwells in the hearts of men'. Here

Carlyle left the world of observable signs, and documentary evidence, and entered the realm of psychological speculation. This interpretation reflected Carlyle's own political philosophy. He was opposed to democratic revolutions, and in favour of authoritarian regimes led by exceptional, strong men. Carlyle believed, as we see here, that most human beings were driven by irrational passions, which needed to be forcibly contained by the state.

Ten years after Carlyle's history appeared in England, the French historian Jules Michelet published his own account of the revolution, offering a radically different interpretation, but one equally steeped in the sentiments of its author. Michelet agreed with Carlyle that the revolution was something that lay deep in human psychology, but for him it was to be found not in madness, rage, or terror, but in the spirit of love and 'universal sympathy' of people for each other. Maximilien Robespierre had suggested the same thing in a speech to the National Assembly at the height of the Terror. The atrabiliar and bespectacled Robespierre described the virtuous feeling that drove the revolution as that 'tender, irresistible, imperious passion, torment, and delight of magnanimous hearts, that profound horror of tyranny, that compassionate zeal for the oppressed', which was ultimately rooted in a 'sublime and sacred love for humanity'.

Looking back today at Carlyle's and Michelet's colourful, personal, and romantic histories of the French Revolution, we see historians gazing down the well of history and seeing reflections of their own feelings. There is an obvious relationship between the authors' emotions, those ascribed to their protagonists, and the ardent political and nationalistic feelings these historians hoped to inspire in their readers. Their successors in the academic discipline of history made more of an effort to detach themselves from their subjects and to keep their own ideological and emotional commitments a little more hidden. So it was that during the 20th century a transition occurred from the composition of emotional histories to the creation of the history of emotions as a distinct and more disciplined approach to the past.

Where psychology wrestles with history

In a pioneering article in 1941, the French historian Lucien Febvre urged his fellow historians to 'plunge into the darkness where psychology wrestles with history'. This was a region where exciting discoveries were waiting to be made. What Febvre had in mind was a vast investigation, he said, a whole new field of enquiry, exploring the history of sensibility and the affective life—in French, *la sensibilité* and *la vie affective*. He wanted historians to create new histories of love and joy, of fear, hatred, and cruelty, in short of all the sentimental and affective dimensions of life and death through the centuries. Febvre pointed to sources and methods that historians could use in this endeavour, such as the study of the history of language and emotional vocabularies, the history of the visual arts, including devotional paintings and sculpture, the role of literature, drama, and film, and the analysis of legal documents and moral treatises. In taking the emotions of the past within its field of view, the discipline of history was promised a whole new beginning, Febvre said: 'What surprises we may look forward to!'

Lucien Febvre was a leading light in what became known as the *Annales* school of history. This group believed in an interdisciplinary approach, linking history with economics, geography, sociology, and psychology. However, from the outset, Febvre was clear that there should be no simple application of 20th-century psychology to earlier historical periods. That was why he used the image of history wrestling with, rather than simply adopting, the theories of psychology. The latter approach has sometimes been attempted by scholars working in the discipline of 'psychohistory', in which a particular theory, such as Freudian psychoanalysis, is used as a template to understand historical individuals. This was not the approach recommended by Febvre in his foundational writings about the history of emotions.

In an essay for the *Encyclopédie française* in 1938, Febvre went so far as to say that the contemporary science of psychology could have 'no possible application to the past', and that psychological anachronism was the most insidious and harmful kind of anachronism. What did he mean by this? Febvre was a forceful writer and had a tendency to use provocative statements to emphasize his ideas. He believed that historians should be familiar with and take an interest in the modern sciences of mind and society. However, his warning against anachronism was important. He was the first historian to see clearly how emotional experiences in the past were complex entities that could only come into existence through the particular social, linguistic, and mental systems that prevailed in a particular period. They were much more than mere reflexes, and crucially they changed over time. Emotions were vehicles of social and psychological meanings made possible only through particular modes of life and thought. As those modes of life and thought changed, the emotions experienced and expressed by people changed.

As Febvre pointed out, modern psychology—a form of scientific study largely based on exploring the feelings and behaviour of affluent, western, white people—could hardly be expected to provide insights into the mental lives of people living in earlier and very different periods. In the past, people's lives were different in many fundamental ways. They lived in a world not yet explained or tamed by modern science and medicine. Life and health hung by a thread, whether through the unpredictability of the climate, or the threat of famine and disease. Communication and travel were, by our standards, incredibly slow, difficult, expensive, and dangerous. Human experience has also been revolutionized by medical inventions such as effective pain relief and contraception. It felt different to live in the world before these extraordinary technologies of control existed. Mental as well as physical conditions have changed radically too. For most of the history of most parts of the world, people have understood their everyday experiences in terms of the influence of supernatural beings—of one God or several deities, with attendant spirits, imps, and demons, assisted by select human beings with special access to cosmic forces of good or evil. To believe that failed crops and diseased livestock could be explained by the displeasure of God or the curse of a witch, rather than by meteorology or animal hygiene, was to live in a different world. The fears and desires of such a world were not just the same emotions that modern psychology studies, but interpreted differently. The interpretation is an integral part of the emotion, and therefore creates a fundamentally different experience.

Another large-scale transition that especially interested historians in the first half of the 20th century was what they saw as the evolution of human cultures from a 'primitive' to a more 'civilized' state. They inherited this way of thinking from evolutionary thinkers in the 19th century, for whom a key measure of increasing civilization in human groups was the restraint and containment of their emotions. In his foundational 1872 book on *The Expression of the Emotions in Man and Animals*, Charles Darwin contrasted the hysterical, child-like weeping and laughing of the 'savages' he had encountered in South America with the emotional restraint of the 'civilized nations of Europe'. An influential work that applied a similar idea to medieval societies was *The Waning of The Middle Ages* by the Dutch historian Johan Huizinga, published in 1919. Huizinga contrasted the highly emotional, volatile, and violent life of the late Middle Ages with the more rational, contained, and civilized nature of modernity. The German sociologist Norbert Elias created yet another, more Freudian, version of this narrative in his 1939 book *The Civilising Process*, according to which medieval people were more wild, cruel, and controlled by their passions because they lacked a stable 'super-ego'.

There are elements of truth in these narratives, including the fact that styles of emotional expression vary from one culture, and one era, to another, and that the rise of the modern nation state, with its drive to centralize and monopolize the use of force, significantly altered how often and at whose hands people might expect to encounter violence. Looking at the wider picture, however, historians from Lucien Febvre onwards have tended to resist the attempt to paint the history of emotions in such primary colours. They have rightly criticized histories that view earlier, and non-European, societies as a whole as 'child-like' or 'primitive' in their experiences and expressions of emotions. The desire to criticize the misleading, and ultimately imperialist nature of the modernist 'civilizing process' narrative was the starting point for many key contributions to the history of emotions when it began to take shape as a recognized area of scholarly endeavour.

It was from the 1980s onwards that the continued wrestling between history and psychology over emotions began to give rise to a whole new field of study. Historian Peter N. Stearns and psychiatrist Carol Z. Stearns co-authored an article entitled 'Emotionology: Clarifying the History of Emotions and Emotional Standards', published in the *American Historical Review* in 1985, which they followed up with a book in 1986, *Anger: The Struggle for Emotional Control in America's History*. Their central concept of 'emotionology' referred to prevailing standards determining which emotions and emotional expressions were deemed acceptable, and which were repressed or struggled against. In the 1990s and 2000s, books and articles by the anthropologist and historian William M. Reddy and the medievalist Barbara H. Rosenwein added further to the foundations of the field. Reddy's work at this time took a particular interest in the operations of emotional speech acts, which he termed 'emotives', in the context of the French Revolution, drawing on cognitive psychology and anthropology alongside historical sources. In 2002, Rosenwein's article 'Worrying about Emotions in History' introduced the idea of 'emotional communities', emphasizing that attitudes to emotions in any particular era were not homogeneous. Rather they varied according to which social groups an individual belonged to, which might include their family, their class, their religion, their neighbourhood, or their nationality. In a single historical period, multiple, overlapping emotional communities exist, with potentially conflicting ideas about emotions and expression.

Through the work of scholars such as Stearns and Stearns, Reddy, and Rosenwein, what had begun as the vision of one French historian in the 1930s and 1940s finally became a recognized historical specialism. During the early 21st century the field expanded rapidly. Research centres were founded in London, Berlin, Australia, and elsewhere. International conferences were plentiful and publications proliferated. A definitive introduction to the growing field by Jan Plamper was published in 2012. In the same year, another German historian, Ute Frevert, Director of the Centre for the History of Emotions at the Max Planck Institute for Human Development, delivered the first in a new annual lecture series devoted to the subject at Queen Mary University of London. There is now also an international Society for the History of Emotions, which has been publishing its journal, *Emotions: History, Culture, Society* since 2017.

So, historians have finally started to make good on Lucien Febvre's promises about the many surprises and rewards that a historical study of the emotions would deliver. But what does this kind of history look like in practice? How do historians know when they have found an emotion in their sources? And what can they usefully say about it? It is easiest to get a handle on these questions by looking at a particular, emotional moment in the past.

Reading a woman's tears: London, 1940

As we begin the attempt to mine historical sources for traces of feeling, an even more fundamental question arises. Is it even possible, we might wonder, for a historian to access something as fleeting, bodily, and subjective as an emotion through dry documents in dusty archives? It is undoubtedly a challenge. However, it is not an unprecedented one. Historians of ideas have long attempted to think again the thoughts of the dead based on the records they left. That is the work of historians of ideas and political thought. To imagine people's emotions is not an entirely different task. Further, the idea that it is hard to access the emotions of the dead implies a contrast with the living, whose emotions we can more easily discover. However, it is not that straightforward. Every day we try to understand those around us by imagining what invisible feelings and emotions might lie behind their outward words and actions. Sometimes we gain insight, sometimes not. We can even be mistaken about our own emotions, when trying to untangle the mess inside. As Lucien Febvre put it in 1941, the attempt to reconstitute the emotional life of the past is 'at one and the same time extremely attractive and frightfully difficult'. Frightfully difficult, but not impossible. In the past, as in the present, there are no unmediated feelings and emotions offering themselves for our inspection. We are always met instead with words, actions, expressions, and images that we can see, from which to infer the feelings we cannot.

Not only are the emotions of the mind invisible, but they rarely operate alone. Any particular emotion exists in a web made of the beliefs, life story, relationships, and cultural education of a particular human being, as well as being entangled with their other emotions. As historians, we will much more often encounter scenarios with multiple emotional dimensions than we will come across a clear example of a single, isolated feeling such as joy or grief. Even a very brief historical account can open up many

1. Bombing raids on London during the Second World War created a range of emotional experiences, including terror, camaraderie, and stoic resolve.

different and fascinating questions about the emotions implied within it. Let us look, then, at an example of such a source—a few lines in a typewritten document, produced in London during the Second World War.

This tiny fragment of the historical record is taken from a report produced in the summer of 1940 by the Mass Observation group. This collective had been set up in 1937 with the aim of producing a record of everyday life in modern Britain in the same way that an anthropologist might document the customs and manners of a distant tribe. As the bombing raids on London and other British cities intensified (see Figure 1), Mass Observation started to produce weekly reports for the government about what they termed 'civilian morale'. One of these featured a list of 'extreme cases of nervousness resulting from air raids', which included a short account of a middle-class woman aged about 40 who lived very close to three houses that had been destroyed in a recent raid. During the day this woman kept saying, 'I can't bear the night. I can't bear the night. Anything like this shouldn't be allowed.' The report continued:

> As it grew dark her state grew worse. Eventually she was trembling so much she could hardly talk. She ran upstairs to the lavatory three times in half an hour. Finally when the warning came she urinated on the spot and burst into tears.

The full description of this woman's reaction takes up just nine lines in a 40-page document, typed on foolscap paper and stapled in the top left-hand corner. How can such an archived feeling be accessed and interpreted by a historian of emotions?

To start with we might ask whether this is an example of an emotion at all. The report included this woman as an example of 'extreme nervousness'. Is that an emotion? It does not seem to be quite the same thing as 'anxiety' or 'terror', although we might assume that such emotions were behind her state. This idea of 'nervousness' had historical roots in medical beliefs about the importance of the nerves which rose to prominence in the 19th century and continued to dominate popular understandings of the mind and body well into the 20th. The terms 'neurosis' and 'neurotic' have the same origins. There was a lucrative market in popular pills and tonics, advertised especially to women, to help them strengthen their nerves and protect against tearful outbursts. So, for the authors of this report, the woman trembling, weeping, and urinating was an example of a pathological, neurotic individual, a threat to collective morale.

We can justifiably treat this source as evidence of a historical emotion, even though that is not exactly how the authors of the report label it. There are at least two reasons for this. First, while it is essential to be careful not to project our own categories back on to the lives and thoughts of past generations, the categories of emotion, emotional response, fear, and terror were all available to the Mass Observation authors, and to their readers and subjects. So, to see things in these terms is not to make use of categories that were unavailable to the authors and subjects of the source. The same Mass Observation report showed an interest in a range of emotional metrics, including 'the ratio of disquiet to cheerfulness' exhibited in men and women of different ages and social classes. This ratio was interpreted in terms of which groups were most 'depressed'. The most cheerful and least depressed group in this case was made up of younger, working-class men.

Secondly, and more fundamentally, one of the main characteristics that has marked mental experiences out as 'emotions', at least since that term was adopted within foundational psychological texts in the late 19th century, is the arousal and expressiveness of the human body. In his 1872 book about emotions, Charles Darwin wrote, 'Most of our emotions are so closely connected with their expression, that they hardly exist if the body remains passive.' This close identification of bodily expressions with emotions was reinforced by the American philosopher and psychologist William James in a famous article entitled 'What is an emotion?', published in the journal *Mind* in 1884. Taking the example of rage, James asked whether one could imagine the state to exist in someone who had no outward signs of it—'no flushing of the face, no dilatation of the nostrils, no clenching of the teeth, no impulse to vigorous action, but in their stead limp muscles, calm breathing, and a placid face?' James's own answer was clear—such a state would not be rage but instead something 'cold-blooded and dispassionate'. No bodily arousal? No emotion. That was the message from the founders of the modern science of emotions. Or, as the lyrics of the popular 1930s song 'I Won't Dance' put it: 'But this feeling isn't purely mental. For Heaven rest us, I'm not asbestos.'

Not just any old bodily arousal counts as an emotion in modern psychology, however. Watering eyes, shaking limbs, or the act of urination are not, on their own, emotions. It is when such responses accompany a mental representation, or belief, that the experience becomes an emotion. One simple way to put this is that emotions are embodied judgements. They are beliefs registered and expressed in our bodily organs. To take an example used by William James, when I see a bear in the forest and run away, that is an emotional experience because it involves both my judgement that I am in mortal danger, and also my bodily reaction—the churning feeling in my viscera, and the behavioural response of fleeing. In the case of the woman suffering 'extreme nervousness' in London in 1940, we can infer—and the report invites us to—that her bodily reaction was a response to her belief that she and her home and loved ones were in danger of being destroyed by a night-time bombing raid, as she had already seen happen to her near neighbours. That combination of beliefs with bodily responses is what made her behaviour emotional.

Because emotions are embodied judgements, the history of emotions is a history of both bodies and ideas. So, first, it takes bodies seriously. This is history with a pulse, and with bowels: a history of blood, sweat, and tears, of laughter, dance, and song. It is a kind of history that asks questions about bodily sensations and feelings in a broad sense. What did it feel like to be cooped up inside a hot, public air-raid shelter on a summer night, with hundreds of your neighbours? What did the air smell like outside, the morning after a bombing raid? How did it feel to walk across a pile of rubble where a friend's house used to stand? What role did particular physical objects, items of clothing, buildings, furnishings, rooms, and spaces, play in giving an emotion its particular embodied flavour?

The bodily side of emotions is, perhaps, the most obvious to us today. To become 'emotional' is usually something visible and physiological. We can see the tears, the trembling hands, the throbbing veins. But the other, equally important, side of emotions is to be seen in the mental ideas they embody. In the case of the tearful woman in 1940 her experience was shot through with beliefs—both about the outside world and about herself. Reading more widely in the Mass Observation archive and other sources reveals that stoicism and resolve were idealized and celebrated national characteristics. In 1940 the artist C. R. W. Nevinson produced a painting of a resolute London child facing down the threat from the skies, entitled *Cockney Stoic; or Camden Town Kids Don't Cry*. To feel one's body giving way to fear in London in 1940 was to experience one's failure to meet the emotional standards of the community. Those kinds of norms and expectations are what historians of emotions have referred to as the 'emotionology' or 'emotional regime' of a particular culture, within the framework of which individual experiences take place. It is important to realize that these rules and expectations form an inherent part of the emotional experience. To take one more example of this—to feel tested by a lust that one believes is a sinful temptation sent by the devil, and which would lead to immoral or criminal acts, is fundamentally different from feeling a kind of sexual desire that one considers a healthy, natural instinct. Our interpretations of our passions and emotions are integral to our emotional experiences; they are neither a veneer nor an afterthought. It's interpretations all the way down.

Thinking and feeling

Some of the most powerful and historically ancient beliefs about emotions are connected with dichotomies of gender, associating some mental states more with women, and others with men. Throughout western history, writers and philosophers have made distinctions between thinking and feeling, the head and the heart, reason and the passions, intellect and emotion. Those contrasts are all subtly different from each other, but the general picture is one that has proved hard to escape, and historically women have been more often associated with emotion, and men with alleged strength of intellect. In the early 1980s, the Black feminist writer Audre Lorde commented that men were still being taught that their domain was understanding and knowledge, while they should 'keep women around to do their feeling for them, like ants do aphids'. For Lorde, this segregation of thought and feeling was harmful both for women, who were thereby excluded from knowledge, understanding, and respect, and also for men, whose repressed feelings lead to pain, hostility, and violence.

There have been several different strategies in trying to overcome this stereotypical contrasting of female feeling with male rationality. In her writings in the 1790s, the English feminist Mary Wollstonecraft argued that women, like men, needed to be properly educated so that their powers of reason and understanding were fully developed, and were thus strong enough to control and guide their passions: women, like men, should be rational beings in command of their feelings. A second strategy is represented by Audre Lorde, who argued that both men and women needed to be fully in touch with their emotions, because 'Our feelings are our most genuine paths to knowledge.' Both Wollstonecraft's and Lorde's approaches maintain a distinction between feeling and understanding, but they try to find new ways to reconnect and revalue the two poles of that contrast, exhorting women to develop their qualities of intellect, or urging men to get in touch with the supposedly feminine domain of feelings.

A third strategy tries to overcome the duality by treating emotions themselves as forms of thought. The American moral philosopher Martha Nussbaum has been a prominent advocate of this view, according to which emotions are a kind of value judgement about the external world, infused with an intelligence and rationality of their own, depending on how accurately they represent the world to us. This is sometimes called the 'cognitive' view, and sometimes the 'neo-Stoic' theory of emotions, since it draws on ideas about the passions going back to ancient Greek and Roman Stoic philosophers. On this view, passions and emotions are opinions or judgements about the world. For instance, my rage is the belief I have been insulted and should take revenge, while my terror is the belief that I am in dire immediate danger.

One final way to mention in which the contrast between rational men and over-emotional women was blurred during the 20th century arose from the experience of modern warfare. The terrible emotional aftermath of the First World War showed that men, as well as women, could suffer from hysteria and extreme nervousness, in the form of 'shell shock'. Of the four cases of 'extreme nervousness' in the Mass Observation report that included the weeping woman, two of the other three were men. One was a butcher who was described as being ill through the air raids: 'He was shell shocked in the last war,' a neighbour reported, 'and apparently he's gone a bit mental.' And as a final note, in the spirit of Martha Nussbaum, we should ask, in any case, how neurotic or irrational such responses really were, whether experienced by women or men. The emotional reaction of terror, as a negative value judgement about the impending possible destruction of one's home by a bombing raid, surely seems quite a rational and intelligent one.

Why study the history of emotions?

People in the past, as in the present, were passionate, full-blooded, human beings, with feelings, longings, sensations, and bodily organs like ours. They sweated and strained, stormed and stressed. They were moved and motivated by their emotions, not just by their thoughts, ideas, or economic and political interests. As such, emotions are important subjects for historians to try to understand and analyse. To make the transition from a historical account that ignores emotions to one that brings them to our attention is a bit like the famous scene near the start of the Hollywood movie *The Wizard of Oz* (1939), when the picture transforms from black and white to glorious technicolour for the first time.

Like all history, the history of emotions is a conversation between the present and the past, and we can hope that the conversation will enhance our understanding of emotions in the present, as well as deepening our knowledge of the past. Emotional traces left in documents, artefacts, and works of art, provide us with a glimpse into worlds of feeling which are at once similar to and different from our own. Like an anthropologist, the historian of emotions tries to reconstruct the beliefs, values, and feelings of a past culture as a counterpoint to their own experience of the world. And that in turn can be a liberating experience. To discover how radically different the interpretations, expressions, and categories of feeling were in the past is to loosen the hold of our contemporary psychological notions over us. Even the idea that there is a distinct category of felt human experiences called 'the emotions' has only been around since the 19th century, and psychologists have never been able to agree on how many 'emotions' there are or what they all have in common. Similarly, studying the history of the relative roles of, say, philosophy, religion, science, and medicine, in shaping beliefs about the mind and its movements, can open our eyes to a much richer set of affective possibilities than the theories of 21st-century psychology might at first seem to allow.

The history of emotions shows us that any particular way of thinking about feelings, past or present, is the product of contingent historical processes. This helps to unsettle the belief that any such picture is inevitable, natural, or universal. One standard psychological approach is to ask what emotions 'we' have, or how 'the brain' works, as if there were a singular answer that would be true for all brains and all humans in all times and places. The history of emotions, by and large, rejects such universalism. And yet the discipline is founded on an assumption, whether explicitly stated or not, of some kind of shared connection between the historian and their subjects. Historians of emotion, in however imperfect a way, do usually hope to help us see inside the minds of the dead. The range of feelings available in the past, while often diverging markedly from our own, are generally part of a recognizable, albeit very large and only partially shared, human repertoire.

An observation about the virtues of travel writing made by the English physician and author Thomas Cogan in the early 19th century makes this point nicely. In his *Philosophical Treatise on the Passions*, Cogan observed that travellers' tales revealed the huge diversity of 'opinions and manners, with their correspondent predilections and aversions' that were found in different parts of the world. He continued:

> They indicate the inconceivable variety of sentiments and affections, which incidentally take place among beings of the same species, inhabitants of the same sublunary system, conversant with similar objects, and possessing similar powers of mind.

The history of emotions has the ability to let us not only see but also feel sameness and difference, connection and distance in relation to our fellow humans. An inconceivable variety of sentiments and affections have moved human bodies and minds in the past. How we feel, and how we think about how we feel, has changed radically, and that change has created new and different emotional experiences. Nonetheless, historians of emotions and their subjects remain beings of the same species, possessing similar powers of mind.

This is a book of two halves. Every chapter, including the present one, looks both at big questions about historical ideas, sources, and methods, and also at particular emotions in the past as case studies. The first three chapters have more of a focus on big ideas—starting with the history, aims, and methods of the history of emotions as a field in this chapter, followed by a survey of the major medical, moral, and scientific theories of feeling and how they have been represented in the arts, through the histories of woe and weeping, and then a chapter on the crucial role of languages, verbal and visual, in categorizing and shaping emotions. The final three chapters then pursue these same issues through case studies of specific families of feeling—terror and happiness taken together, rage, and finally love—sampling the growing body of research historians of emotions have produced showing how human experiences have changed through the centuries.

That may all sound rather abstract, but hopefully in what follows the concrete value of the history of emotions will become obvious, as a way to think about some very particular issues. For instance, a historical approach is essential in thinking about whether 'depression' is the name of an emotion, a clinical disorder, or both. We can look at how the concept of depression today relates to earlier ideas about *melancholia* and black bile, and what its expanding domain tells us about the roles of medicine and psychiatry in modern history. Similarly, paying attention to the differences between 'passions of the soul' and modern 'emotions' forces us to think critically about whether we really believe our emotions are all 'natural' and 'valid' and what we might mean by saying that. As we have already seen, the history of emotions can contribute to conversations about gender politics too. Are ideas about women being more tearful and men more aggressive, for instance, cultural constructs or universal truths? And when and why did people start to argue that it would be good for men to cry and women to express their rage? Twenty-first-century movements including #MeToo, Black Lives Matter, and Extinction Rebellion invite conversations about the histories of anger, compassion, and joy as emotions of protest and activism. Finally, history will help us ask whether the cherished—and apparently emotional—states of happiness and love are really emotions at all.

Chapter 2
A map of woe

Above my desk hangs a print by the artist Aidan Moesby. At first glance it looks like a copy of the famous periodic table of 118 chemical elements, each represented by a one- or two-letter abbreviation, in its own little square. On closer inspection, however, it transpires that the squares contain not elements but emotions, each with its own abbreviation and the equivalent of an atomic number. So, for instance, in the place of hydrogen (H), with atomic number 1, is happy (Hy). Carbon (C) is replaced by bleak (Bl), and polonium (Po), number 84 in the chemical table, becomes fury (Fu) in the emotional one. Colour is used to group related emotions together in families of feelings with a shared theme, such as happiness, anger, or love. One morally charged grouping is made up of the seven deadly sins of traditional Christian teaching, and their countervailing virtues (see Figure 2).

The largest family of emotions in the table is a collection of 18 depressed mental states, coloured in blue: low, bleak, worried, sad, miserable, desperate, sombre, sorrowful, dejected, subdued, demoralized, empty, unhappy, morose, desolate, awful, dreadful, and suicidal. One could of course think of even more words to add to this lexicon of woe. Related emotion words including 'melancholic', 'abandoned', and 'crushed' appear in other parts of the table. What I especially like about Moesby's image, entitled 'Sagacity', is the way that it captures both the scientific aspiration

The History of Emotions

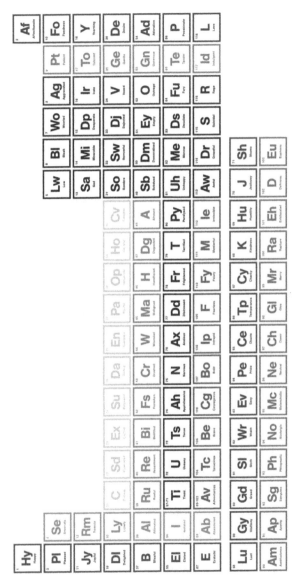

2. Aidan Moesby's 'Sagacity' print (2015) alludes both to the wide range of the emotional lexicon and to the human desire to put feelings in boxes.

to reduce human emotions to a limited and manageable number that can be treated as universal, and also the impossibility of doing so. Even 118 English words can only plot some of the most notable features in the wide, dramatic terrain of human feeling, and their inclusion immediately brings to mind many more emotional landmarks, not recorded on this particular map.

Moesby's periodic table of emotions gets us thinking about science, language, and the attempt to define and name our feelings. It alludes simultaneously to the reductive aims of modern science and to rich historical languages of feeling. The interaction between science and art mirrors the dual nature of emotions as both physiological and cultural. All our emotions are produced by a body and a historically situated culture working together. If one of the partners is missing, the results are no longer emotions, but either mere physiological reflexes or disembodied representations. Both the performers in this complex dance of body and culture have changed over time, and this is illustrated nowhere more vividly than in the histories of sadness, grief, melancholy, and depression.

A basic emotion?

One of the most influential recent cultural representations of sadness was as a tearful blue cartoon character in the 2015 movie *Inside Out*. The film won the award for best animated feature at both the Oscars and the Golden Globes, and internationally went on to earn an estimated $858m. Outside its home market in North America, it has been successful in the United Kingdom, Japan, South Korea, Germany, and France. I know from my own experience visiting schools in England that displays featuring the five main characters in the film—the emotions that control the brain of the film's protagonist, Riley—are among the most popular ways of teaching young children about feelings today. In fact, it is hard to think of any representation of human emotions that has had more international influence in the 21st century. So, what theory of emotions is the film based on, and what ideas about sadness might viewers take away from it?

Inside Out tells the story of 11-year-old Riley who has moved from Minnesota to San Francisco and is desperately missing her old life. It takes its title from the fact that we see the action unfold from two perspectives—one inside Riley's brain, and the other in her outer life, interacting with her parents, going to school, and eventually deciding to run away to return to her old home. The emphasis is very much on the 'inside' part of the title, as the five emotions in Riley's brain endeavour to influence her behaviour. The lead character is Joy, and she is joined by Disgust, Fear, Anger, and Sadness in the attempt to guide Riley towards her goals. Among the qualities of the film is the rich metaphorical landscape it conjures up to depict Riley's mind—including islands of personality and a vast physical storehouse of memories, represented by glowing glass bowling balls that change colour depending on their emotional tone. There are tubes, wires, and even a 'train of thought', connecting up the different regions. As the emotions navigate this landscape, it is the character of Sadness who becomes central. The take-home message of the film is that sadness is a normal part of every human life, closely involved with cherished memories and key family relationships, and integral to the very possibility of joy.

Inside Out has an additional importance in the history of ideas about emotions. It represents a stage—perhaps the all-time high-point—in the influence of one particular psychological theory. This is the theory of 'basic emotions', developed and popularized with huge success by the American psychologist Paul Ekman and others since the 1970s—a universalist view of emotions as hardwired mental states, which originally evolved for specific purposes in ancestral humans. Theorists have disagreed about the name and number of these 'basic emotions', and Ekman himself in his later work expanded the list quite substantially, from an initial count of seven (the five from *Inside Out* plus surprise and contempt), to a longer list of 15, including amusement, embarrassment, guilt, shame, pride in achievement, relief, and others.

What basic-emotion theorists share is the belief that there is a limited number of emotions, the same across all cultures, which evolved as physiological states to help our ancestors deal with a range of scenarios, such as danger, threat, loss, and the pursuit of their goals. On this view, each emotion puts the body into a mode of readiness appropriate to the circumstances, while simultaneously signalling the feeling to others through a distinctive facial expression. The theory treats our emotions as hardwired survival mechanisms. When faced with a threat, our aggressive fighting instinct kicks in; if we accidentally eat rotten food, we are protected from it by our feeling of disgust, making us spit it out or vomit. Even though most of us now live lives very different from those of our evolutionary ancestors, this theory suggests we have the same emotional tool kit they did. The story of Riley and her five emotions is a version of this basic-emotions theory, and Paul Ekman was among the psychologists consulted by the director of *Inside Out*, Pete Docter, during the research and development for the film.

The idea that all human feeling and behaviour can be explained by the influence of a small number of basic emotions, pulling the levers inside our brains, may be a good starting point for young children learning their first emotion words. It might also be a useful scientific hypothesis in some contexts. We surely do have inherited instincts, but most of our emotions, including those of misery and sorrow, seem too elaborate and too cultural to be understood as a kind of triggered reflex. History reinforces this impression. While adversity, suffering, and death have always been universals of human life, the emotions and expressions they elicit are not. Studying the social and cultural histories of these evolving feelings can help us produce more nuanced, more accurate, and more therapeutic maps of woe. Indeed, people have long turned to history as a way to help them construct such maps, including William Shakespeare when he decided to stage the story of a woeful Roman general for audiences at the end of the 16th century.

The woefull'st man that ever lived in Rome

Today we often consume emotional dramas via our screens—tears and movies sometimes streaming simultaneously. For our ancestors in the 16th and 17th centuries, similar experiences were to be had attending live performances in playhouses. Renaissance tragedies followed classical models, and their emotional function remained the same as it had been in ancient Greece and Rome—to elicit terror and pity in response to the drama, and to provide stories and images with which people could think about their own feelings. In Shakespeare's *Lamentable Roman Tragedy of Titus Andronicus*, the terror was produced by extreme, gory violence, and the pity by tragic deaths and grieving, while the audience was offered a rich representation of tears and sorrows in a range of images. In the play, the human body is both a system of signs and also a vessel filled with, and animated by, vital fluids connecting its emotions with physical nature.

Titus Andronicus centres around the rape and mutilation of Titus' daughter Lavinia, the murder of her husband, and the framing and execution of two of her brothers for both crimes. The play offers insights into a range of Renaissance understandings of the mind and body. First, there is the way that the body itself is interpreted as a kind of legible, emotional text. After Lavinia's and Titus' mutilations—she has lost both hands, and her tongue, he has lost one hand—Titus sits with his daughter and reflects on their limited ability to express themselves. Without our hands, he says, we 'cannot passionate our tenfold grief'. Then he addresses Lavinia directly, saying, 'Thou map of woe, that thus dost talk in signs!' Titus promises to learn the meanings of her tears and sighs, and of the raising of her stumps to heaven, making an alphabet of grief from 'her martyr'd signs'. This depiction of the human body as a document—a map that can be read and decoded as a guide to the thoughts of each character—makes *Titus Andronicus* a play which is more outside-in than *Inside Out*.

The picture of feeling and expression that Shakespeare paints makes human passions continuous with other natural forces. In the speech that Titus delivers at the peak of his sorrowing over the violence committed against his daughter, he identifies himself with the ocean of sorrows that surrounds him, at the same time describing Lavinia as the wind and sky—or 'welkin':

> I am the sea; hark how her sighs do blow!
> She is the weeping welkin, I the earth:
> Then must my sea be moved with her sighs;
> Then must my earth with her continual tears
> Become a deluge, overflow'd and drown'd

Shakespeare deploys other natural images too in his portrayal of the tears of Titus and his family, describing them as streams, rivers, oceans, storms, and rain-showers. Titus' grandson is described as a tender sapling and his grandfather tells him, 'thou are made of tears'. According to Renaissance medical theory, children, like women and old men, were naturally more prone to tears. Women were thought of as 'leaky vessels', and their tears flowed from them as natural fluids, alongside breast milk and menstrual blood, while men became in some ways more feminine as they aged, including their propensity for weeping.

Finally, the text of *Titus Andronicus* includes a couple of indications of the original meaning of the word 'sad'. In its Anglo-Saxon, Norse, and Latin roots, 'sad' meant gorged with food, sated, or full. To be 'sad' in this sense was literally to be 'fed up'—to have had enough, or indeed more than enough. Titus, 'the woefull'st man that ever lived in Rome', was full to overflowing with woes and tears. He says of Lavinia, 'For why my bowels

cannot hide her woes, But like a drunkard must I vomit them.'
Extending this sense of being over-full, 'sad' also came to mean
heavy. A French–English dictionary of 1611 translated the French
Fromage de taulpe as 'heavy or sad cheese'. When Titus' grandson
Lucius is distressed by the old man's sorrows, Titus' brother
comments: 'Alas, the tender boy, in passion moved, Doth weep to
see his grandsire's heaviness.'

The sad tears of the sorrowing and grieving characters in *Titus
Andronicus* operated as both signs and secretions. As such they
could be interpreted either by a moral theory of the passions or by
a medical understanding of the body, especially of what the
scholar and writer Robert Burton would call 'the liquid or fluent
part of the body'. That was a phrase he used in 1621, in the longest
and most famous book about 'melancholy' ever published. To
understand more about the longer history of that term and its
place in Renaissance medicine and culture, we can turn to the
world of Burton and his book.

Black bile

Robert Burton was a bookish, idiosyncratic, and melancholic
Oxford clergyman. The full title of his great work was *The
Anatomy of Melancholy, What it is: With all the Kinds, Causes,
Symptomes, Prognostickes, and Several Cures of it. In Three Maine
Partitions with their several Sections, Members, and Subsections.
Philosophically, Medicinally, Historically, Opened and Cut Up*
(see Figure 3). Modern paperback editions run to over 1,300
pages. It has been described as one of the greatest, most amusing,
and most original works in the English language, despite the fact
that hardly anyone can claim to have read the whole thing. It
offers a panoramic view of the place of melancholy in an early
modern world of passions, temperaments, medicine, and morality.

Three of the key forms of melancholy that Burton's text picked out
for examination were a transitory feeling, a chronic disease, and a

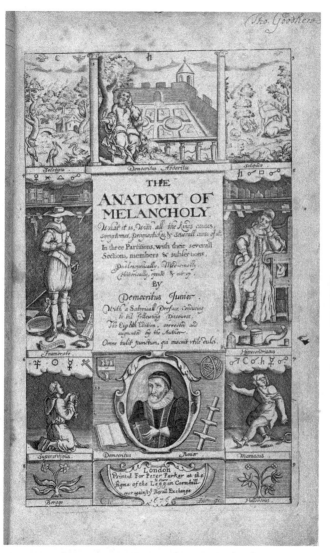

3. The frontispiece of Robert Burton's *Anatomy of Melancholy* depicted figures of lovesick, hypochondriacal, superstitious, and manic melancholy.

universal madness. The first species of melancholy was what we might today identify as a temporary emotional reaction, described by Burton as:

> that transitory melancholy which goes and comes upon every small occasion of sorrow, need, sickness, trouble, fear, grief, passion, or perturbation of the mind, any manner of care, discontent, or thought, which causeth anguish, dullness, heaviness and vexation of spirit.

For Burton, such feelings of anguish and grief were a universal part of human life, and he distinguished them from the second kind of melancholy, which he claimed was his true subject, namely melancholy which was a habit, a chronic disease, or a 'settled humour' suffered only by some, due to their temperament. Finally, however, in another sense 'melancholy' functioned as a term for almost any kind of foolishness or mental disorder, which again broadened the term's domain so that it became universal: 'all the world is melancholy, or mad'.

In its hundreds upon hundreds of pages, Burton's *Anatomy* uses countless quotations, drawn from ancient, medieval, and early modern texts. This material is held together by the underpinning ancient medical model of the four humours, from which the very term 'melancholy' derived. According to ancient Greek medicine, the body was filled and animated by four vital fluids, or 'humours': blood, phlegm, yellow bile, and black bile. Yellow bile was sometimes called 'choler', and black bile was known as 'black choler' or 'melancholy', the latter being the Anglicized version of the Greek *melancholia*. According to humoral medicine, the four humours needed to be kept in balance and an excess of any one of them led to distinctive bodily types, personalities, and illnesses, including melancholic ones.

Early modern people experiencing either transitory feelings of grief and heaviness or more long-lasting and perturbing ones of dread and sorrow felt in their souls and bodies the effects of excessive black bile, and thought about how they might rebalance their humours to alleviate its effects. The cures they turned to included herbal and medicinal ones, and also activities that would still be recognized today as sensible ones to engage in to raise one's spirits, such as going for a walk in nature, reading books and poetry, playing music, laughing, and spending time with friends. On the final page of the *Anatomy*, Burton offers some pithy advice which would not be out of place in a modern self-help book. If you care about your physical and mental health, Burton recommends, you should follow this short precept: 'Be not solitary, be not idle.'

That aphorism is not quite the end of Burton's book, however, and the way it does end reminds us that we are not, in fact, reading a modern self-help book. The closing lines are quotations in Latin which look beyond the medical world to things eternal. The first of these is the phrase '*Sperate miseri, Cavete felices*', meaning that the miserable should have hope and the happy beware. The implication here is that a feeling of misery indicates an apt sense of one's sinful nature and the need for urgent repentance, as opposed to an unwise moral complacency. And the final word of the *Anatomy* is given to St Augustine, the North African theologian who became Bishop of Hippo in 395 CE. The quotation from Augustine advises Christians that they would do well to spend their time reflecting on and repenting of their sins, since while engaged in such penitence they will not be committing any more sins. This Renaissance compendium of feelings, then, ends with a piece of early medieval spiritual advice about the benefits of godly sorrow—a form of religious emotion that could be expressed through both the soul and the body.

The gift of tears

Augustine of Hippo's extraordinary autobiographical *Confessions* offers a glimpse into the emotional life of a newly converted Christian in Roman North Africa at the end of the 4th century.

Augustine was a man of strong and varied passions, who, by his own account, had turned away from a life of lust and sensual pleasures in search of a more lasting, spiritual joy. His thinking about feeling went on to have a huge influence on medieval Christian teaching. It represented both a new interpretation of biblical views of emotion, and also a critical commentary on classical philosophers, especially the Stoics, who valued calm, dispassionate wisdom above all, and frowned on those who seemed to be slaves to their passions. For Augustine, the path from the earthly city to *The City of God* (the title of another of his major works) was an emotional one. It was not a route that human beings could expect to tread without suffering, sorrow, and tears.

Although tears can be shed under the influence of many emotions, including joy and rage, or for purely physical reasons, they have historically been most frequently associated with grief and sorrow, as they were by Augustine. The record of his response to the death of his mother, Monica, offers an example of how Augustine applied his ideas about such emotions to his own life. Monica was not only Augustine's mother but also the person who brought him to Christianity. Addressing himself to God, in *The Confessions*, Augustine recalled that, although he had been holding back his grief in public, when he was alone he suddenly felt with a new force the memories of the tenderness and patience his mother had shown him:

> Of all this I found myself suddenly deprived, and it was a comfort to me to weep for her and for myself and to offer my tears to you for her sake and for mine. The tears which I had been holding back streamed down, and I let them flow as freely as they would, making of them a pillow for my heart.

Augustine went on to comment that some might have despised and mocked him for weeping for his mother, considering it a sin to show grief rather than joy when Monica was reunited with God in heaven. Of such a critic, Augustine said: 'Let him not mock at me but weep himself, if his charity is great. Let him weep for my sins to you, the Father of all.' In other words, tears of grief for the faithful departed may have been, strictly speaking, theologically suspect, but they were eminently human, and should elicit understanding and compassion in others rather than condemnation.

Medieval religious teaching generally echoed these sentiments, recommending godly sorrow and the gift of tears as valuable parts of the spiritual life. A later handbook of Christian weeping taught that there were three appropriate kinds of crying—tears of devotion, of compassion, and of compunction. Someone blessed with the gift of tears might, then, shed them to express their devotion to God, their compassion for the suffering of others, or their compunction for their own sins. 'Compunction' here had a dual meaning of sorrowful repentance for wrong-doing and also a kind of spiritual puncturing or piercing, resulting in a flow of both tears and penitence. Biblical accounts of Jesus shedding tears, and representations in religious sculptures and paintings of the tears of the Virgin Mary (see Figure 4) and Mary Magdalene weeping over the crucified Christ, all provided models of godly sorrow for believers to follow. Some extravagant examples of this kind of spiritual weeping are to be found in the lives of female mystics of the Middle Ages, most famously in the autobiographical writing of the miller, brewer, and religious visionary Margery Kempe, whose later life was a story of pilgrimages of tears, from England to the Holy Land and back again.

During the Reformation in Europe in the 16th and 17th centuries, tears and grief were reassessed once more. Protestants attacked the Catholic cult of tears, grief, and wailing for the dead. The Catholic belief that the souls of the dead could be helped through purgatory by the tears of earthly mourners seemed to offer too much agency to the emotions of sinful humans, and to detract from the power of God to decide the fate of the souls of the

4. This 15th-century painting of the Virgin Mary as the 'Mater Dolorosa', or grieving mother, by the workshop of Dieric Bouts is an example of how works of religious art were used to model and inspire emotional responses.

departed. Comparable disagreements took place in other religions too. Although the Qu'rān includes several references to weeping, including the tears of the Prophet Muhammad himself, doctrinal conflicts continued about whether emotional expressions of grief were acceptable within Islamic rituals. The Mourning of Muharram is an annual ritual, commemorating the death of the grandson of Muhammad at the Battle of Karbala in 680 CE. Shia Muslims and followers of Sufism have traditionally engaged in more emotional displays of sorrow at this festival, while Sunnis have been more suspicious of public lamentations and have tended to mark the occasion through fasting rather than displays of grief.

The histories of grief and weeping in religious contexts reveal several recurring themes. The first is a recognition that tears and sorrow are understandable responses to universal experiences of loss, adversity, and death. However, religions have tried to put limits on these very human responses. This has sometimes been for theological reasons, according to which faith in God, and resignation to His will, should overcome human feelings of grief. At other times, though, there has been a more political concern, namely the fear that extravagant public performances of mourning will spill over into civil unrest. Emotional acts of remembrance can follow the pattern played out in classical tragedies like *Titus Andronicus*, with grief and mourning transmuting into violent vengeance. Tears are powerful symbols because of their association not just with gentle feelings of sorrow but also with instincts of protest and revolt.

Tears can be sinful or virtuous, self-indulgent or compassionate, conciliatory or divisive. They can also be either healthy or pathological. Even though many cultures have considered tears effeminate or childish, especially if shed in public or to excess, that has generally been accompanied by a belief that, in moderation, tears are a sign of the healthy functioning of body and mind, for both men and women. Indeed, in both ancient and modern sources we encounter the idea that the most dangerous and pathological form of grief is one in which the tears dry up completely. That was the fate of Titus Andronicus, whose emotional journey took him from tearful grief to dry-eyed, violent madness. And in the movie *Inside Out*, Riley's darkest moment is not when she is most sad, but rather when she suffers something beyond that—a kind of complete emotional shut-down. It is when Sadness is able to take over the controls again, and Riley sheds tears in front of her parents, that the mental wounds can start to heal. Tears, it seems, can be a psychological, as well as a spiritual gift.

The most miserable form of insanity

There is a long tradition of finding something of value in human misery. Renaissance and early modern culture forged a strong association between melancholy, intellect, and creativity. We might think of the cliché of the tortured, heroic Romantic poet, splitting his time between misery and mountaineering, or the self-destructive genius in the visual arts, producing beauty out of suffering through a kind of emotional alchemy. Some feel that a depressive view of the world is not only creative but also more truthful. People are terrible. Life is short. We all die. To use the poetic 16th-century language of the burial service of the Church of England, 'Man that is borne of a womanne, hath but a shorte time to lyve, and is full of misery.'

No one doubts that, as viewers of *Inside Out* are encouraged to realize, there is an important place for sad feelings in everyday life. However, sometimes emotional heaviness can become an unbearable burden. Ever since ancient times, some kinds of sorrow have been considered unhealthy, pathological, or sinful. Stoics believed that almost all forms of human feeling were diseases of the soul. In Christianity, while tears and sorrow could be godly, there were other kinds of grief and dejection that were thought to reveal a spiritual malaise or sinfulness. Early Christian lists of 'evil thoughts' and 'deadly sins' included 'acedia'—a feverish, demonic despair suffered especially by solitary monks and nuns—and 'sloth', which somewhat resembled the listlessness of depression, although interpreted within a moral framework as a blameworthy lack of spiritual exertion. Ancient and Renaissance ideas about 'melancholy' similarly spread themselves across both medical and emotional terrains. As we saw in the case of Burton, the word could name a temporary emotion, an inborn temperament, or a universal malady.

By the 19th century, ancient ideas about 'black bile' had been displaced, and scientific understandings of the mind now had the brain and nervous system, rather than the four humours, at their centre. At the same time the language of 'melancholy' and 'melancholia' was gradually displaced by our modern category of 'depression'—a word that already had multiple meanings when it came into use as a standard term for pathological low mood. 'Depression' continues to carry with it a range of geographical, meteorological, emotional, and even social and economic meanings, as well as psychiatric ones. This huge semantic range can lead to disagreements about when a feeling of 'depression' should be considered an everyday emotion and when a sign of mental illness. Since we can legitimately use the language of 'depression' for both of these, and since there has never been a definitive distinction between healthy and unhealthy emotions, this ambiguity is inevitable, perhaps even appropriate.

Some of the fluidity and ambiguity of the language of 'depression' is evident in an early use of the term in a modern sense in 1820. The Scottish physician and philosopher Thomas Brown distinguished, in his lectures on the human mind, between three related but different states of sadness. The first two were different senses of 'melancholy', not much different from Burton's uses of the term 200 years earlier: as a passing emotional response to calamity, or as a lasting feeling which some experience for most of their lives for no discernible reason. We might think the latter was equivalent to modern 'depression'. However, Brown distinguished both his kinds of melancholy from a third state:

that *extreme depression*, which constitutes the most miserable form of insanity, the most miserable disease,—that fixed and deadly gloom of soul, to which there is no sunshine in the summer sky,—no verdure or blossom in the summer field,—no kindness in affection, no purity in the very remembrance of innocence itself—no Heaven, but hell,—no God, but a demon of wrath.

Brown's comments in 1820 reveal the state of flux that emotional language was in at that time. His language is modern in some senses. He is describing a 'form of insanity' and a 'miserable disease', which sounds quite similar to 'clinical depression' today, and yet he also still uses the term 'melancholy' to name a similar inborn state of low mood, and his references to the soul, hell, and 'a demon of wrath' show the strong continued influence of moral and religious imagery.

In the two centuries since Brown lectured students of the mind in Edinburgh, our languages and theories of depression have continued to evolve, reflecting changes both in medical belief and in social attitudes. Dominant therapeutic approaches have transitioned from Victorian medical psychiatry, through the heyday of psychoanalysis in the middle decades of the 20th century, followed by cognitive behavioural therapy (CBT), and finally the dizzyingly rapid rise of a pharmaceutical approach characterized by mass prescriptions of anti-depressant medications, including selective serotonin reuptake inhibitors, or SSRIs, since the 1980s. Prozac was the brand name of one of the most widely prescribed SSRIs in North America and elsewhere, and came to define the era. The psychiatrist Peter Kramer's *Listening to Prozac* came out in 1993, expressing a cautious enthusiasm for the new treatment, and the following year saw the success of Elizabeth Wurtzel's memoir *Prozac Nation*, which later became a movie of the same name, reflecting the sense that this medication was taking over America. SSRIs remain the most commonly prescribed treatment for depression (and other conditions) worldwide, while debates continue about their effectiveness, the reality of the 'chemical imbalance' that SSRIs are supposed to address, the dangers of dependency, and the question of whether anti-depressants are seeking to cure a social ill through pharmaceutical means. The most recent innovations in psychiatric thought have taken a 'trauma-informed' approach, exploring the lasting emotional impact of adverse childhood experiences of neglect, discrimination, and abuse.

From the point of view of the history of emotions, these 20th- and 21st-century developments continue a process that is as old as human culture, of renaming and reframing our feelings. There is no fixed point, but rather an ever-evolving landscape of shifting categories and attitudes, changing causal stories, and new types of treatment. Even in a single community at a particular moment in time, there will be no single agreed meaning for expansive terms like 'sadness' or 'depression'. Nor is there just one kind of depressed emotional state which, when taken to an extreme, is understood to become an illness. For some, the experience of depression is like an extended and profound grief or sadness, but for others it is more like a blank emotional deadness, sometimes referred to as 'anhedonia'. We should perhaps talk about 'sadnesses', 'woes', or 'depressions' in the plural.

This historical realization helps to warn against the idea that there is something fixed called 'depression', or 'clinical depression', which can be understood as a fact of 'brain chemistry', which is either completely present or entirely absent, whether in ourselves or in the historical figures we study. Emotions embody within them their subjects' own beliefs. Painful feelings can be experienced as a passing low mood, or as a sad fact about their inborn temperament by some, or as a symptom of an illness, or of a spiritual crisis by others. Without doubting the value of the efforts of anti-stigma campaigns seeking parity of esteem between mental and physical health conditions, living with a mental syndrome like 'depression' is not, in fact, very much like having a broken leg. You cannot put a depressed person in a scanner to see if they have a mental fracture or not. Legs do not get broken by false beliefs about our legs, nor can they be fixed by talking about what happened to our legs in childhood. There is no significant medical disagreement about how best to fix a broken leg. Emotional disorders, like all emotional experiences, are more fluid and difficult to map than physical ones.

As the American band R.E.M. sang in the 1990s, 'Everybody hurts sometimes.' But that hurt comes in many different forms. History suggests that any attempt to find a single, simple definition of 'hurt' or 'sadness', 'melancholy' or 'depression' is as doomed to failure as the quest for a hardwired biological marker for such conditions. States of heaviness, woe, and sorrow range from the pain of mourning and bereavement after the death of a loved one, to the disappointment of thwarted desires, to the breaking of a bond of romance or friendship, to more diffuse feelings such as hopelessness, despair, or lamentation over the state of the world and humanity. Feelings in this family are present in all human cultures and, although we cannot reduce them to a single universal state, we can learn from history when making new maps of woe to help us navigate our way through them.

Chapter 3
From passions to emojis

On 20 January 2022, the singer Adele uploaded a video post to her Instagram account to say she was cancelling a residency that was due to start at the luxury Caesars Palace hotel in Las Vegas the following day. 'I'm so sorry, but my show ain't ready,' Adele says, looking distressed, distracted, and red-eyed, and citing Covid disruption as the reason. 'I'm gutted, I'm gutted, and I'm sorry it's so last minute,' she explains, pausing to sniff and wipe her nose. 'I'm so upset, and I'm really embarrassed, and I'm so sorry to everyone that's travelled again.' At this point Adele's face crumples. She sighs and blows out her cheeks, seeming to fight back tears, before apologizing over and over in a trembling voice and promising to reschedule the shows. A few words of text accompany the video promising more information soon, along with a single, red broken-heart emoji. Within 12 hours this emotional post had been viewed over eight million times.

Although Adele's apology is not perhaps an event of world-historical significance, it is an interesting example of how emotions can be performed via social media in the 21st century, and a helpful introduction to the history of verbal and visual languages of emotion. We might imagine a future historian taking an eager interest in the video, wondering what it reveals about the emotional conventions and languages of the 2020s. They might think about the way it uses the public ritual of a tearful apology to convey the depth of the singer's regret to potentially angry fans, who had paid a lot for their travel and tickets, and how this emotional performance in turn had a distinctly rational commercial purpose, namely to limit the damage done to Adele as a brand. Our future historian of emotions would also need to figure out the meaning of Adele's words. She uses at least four different phrases to represent her emotional state: 'I'm so sorry,' 'I'm gutted,' 'I'm so upset,' 'I'm really embarrassed.'

Hopefully our future researcher will have access to the *Oxford English Dictionary* (*OED*), and so will be able to study the historical uses of Adele's words. If so, they will discover the surprising fact that the word 'sorry' is descended not from the emotional term 'sorrow', but from northern European terms meaning physically sore, ill, spotty, or scabby. To be 'sorry' in this sense was to be covered in sores, rather than to feel sad. English-speaking people have been feeling 'embarrassed' since around the 1750s. An early use of the term describes a self-conscious monk taking a woman's hand in a sentimental novel called *The Memoirs of a Young Lady of Quality*. The *OED*'s earliest example of 'upset' in the emotional sense comes from one Captain Blackwood in 1805 who was never 'so shocked or so completely upset' as when he heard of the death of Nelson at the battle of Trafalgar. The most recently coined of Adele's emotion words—'gutted'—would be unfamiliar even to many native speakers of English. It is a British slang term, meaning devastated or bitterly disappointed, first used in the 1970s, although echoing long-standing historical connections between emotional feelings and the bowels.

Words for feelings

Although everyday users of any language are generally unaware of the deep cultural and semantic histories contained in their emotional vocabularies, those ancestries are very important to historians of emotions. They help us to track when particular emotion terms began or ceased to be available to people as ways to label, interpret, and talk about their feelings. It is not surprising, therefore, that some historians of emotions have focused very closely on the histories of words as a way of chronicling emotional change. In an important essay on the history of 'nostalgia'—a term first coined in 1688—the Swiss scholar Jean Starobinski went so far as to suggest that the history of emotions 'cannot be anything other than the history of those words in which the emotion is expressed'.

Starobinski was writing in the 1960s, before the history of emotions had emerged as an academic field. Most historians of emotions today would stop short of claiming that the history of emotions can only be a history of words. Work in the field has amply demonstrated the potential for physical objects—from handkerchiefs, jewellery, or bedsheets to furniture, architecture, and works of visual art—to act as sources of information about past emotions and their expressions. Such objects speak to us most clearly, however, when they can be attached to the lives, thoughts, beliefs, and desires of the people who used, owned, exchanged, and bequeathed them. And in attempting to make those connections, we are almost always taken back to contemporary textual sources and the need to interpret their language. Historians of emotions have therefore laboured to reconstruct the emotional vocabularies of the past, asking when key emotional terms fell out of use, remained in use but changed their meaning, or were introduced for the first time. Words are powerful witnesses to social and emotional change.

The painfully lethargic state of 'acedia', which tormented solitary monks in the early middle ages, is one often-used example of a 'lost emotion' that does not feature in modern repertoires of feelings. Among the many terms that have not disappeared from view, but have changed their meaning across time, we might include the one studied by Starobinksi—'nostalgia'—which started life as a medical term for a kind of home-sickness. This original 'nostalgia' was not a gentle emotional feeling, but a potentially deadly mental and physical illness. In her research into 'nostalgia' during the American Civil War, Susan Matt found thousands of cases of the disease documented in medical records. One army surgeon in 1861 wrote that deaths from this cause were 'very frequent', including one recent case in his regiment: 'The poor fellow died of Nostalgia (home-sickness), raving to the last breath about wife and children.' It was only in the 20th century that 'nostalgia' started to mean a sentimental and rose-tinted longing for the past. In addition to emotional words that have dropped out of use or changed their meanings, historians have tracked the introduction of neologisms into the emotional lexicon, many of which have been bequeathed to us by modern science and medicine, such as 'altruism' and 'empathy' in the 19th century, along with a whole range of instincts, manias, phobias, complexes, and disorders. Some terms have been formed on a medical model but taken out of that context to describe cultural or political phenomena too, such as 'Beatlemania' or 'Islamophobia'.

Speech acts and verbal communities

'But,' I hear you object, 'words are not feelings! Language may be important, but the history of emotions must surely be more than a history of words! I don't want to spend my time just looking up feeling words in old dictionaries!' 'Yes, yes,' I reply, 'calm down!' Your exclamations, my response, and also Adele's emotional apology on Instagram saying how upset and gutted she is, are all examples of what philosophers of language call 'performative speech acts', or just 'performatives'. In other words, they are utterances which are not intended to convey factual information, in the manner of a bald factual statement such as 'Beijing is the capital of China.' Instead a performative's main aim is to modify the thoughts and behaviour of other people.

Performative speech acts come in many different forms, including proposals, vows, congratulations, warnings, arrests, verdicts, and apologies: 'Will you marry me?', 'I will,' 'Well done!', 'Look out!', 'I am arresting you on suspicion of serious fraud', 'Guilty,' 'I'm sorry.' Whether in formal legal contexts or everyday life, speech acts can change the world. The anthropologist and historian William Reddy has pointed out that there is a particular subset of speech acts directly concerned with the emotions. Reddy calls these linguistic acts 'emotives', and historians might encounter them in various forms, whether spoken aloud and later written down, or in a private letter, diary, or other document.

As an example of how emotives can affect the emotional state of the speaker as well as the listener, Reddy mentions the English philosopher Bertrand Russell who, a few days after declaring his love to Lady Ottoline Morrell in March 1911, wrote to her,

> I did not know I loved you until I heard myself telling you so—for one instant I thought 'Good God, what have I said?' and then I knew it was the truth.

The same idea can be extended to other emotions. To say 'I am terrified'—or indeed 'I have no fear'—in a time of danger, may partly be a report of an internal state of mind, but it is also an invitation to those hearing or reading the words to act in a particular way, whether offering comfort or, alternatively, issuing an invitation to emulate the speaker's resilience. And, as in the case of Russell's declaration of love, a spoken claim about fear, or indeed any other emotion, might clarify, intensify, transform, or even invert the speaker's own emotional state. To give one final example, to say 'I'm so sorry' may on the surface look like a report of a state of regretful feeling, but again it has a performative function. It is an appeal to others to understand and look kindly on the speaker and forgive them for whatever action or omission they are apologizing for. It is a plea for mercy as much as it is a psychological self-report. The concept of 'emotives' helps historians spot the social work that emotion language is doing.

The idea of an 'emotional community' also encourages us to look at how emotional language has worked in the past. The medievalist Barbara Rosenwein proposed this term to explore how social groups in history—whether families, neighbourhoods, societies, religious orders, military regiments, or professions—have shared their attitudes to emotions and expression. Within any particular community, which could range in size from a close friendship of two people to a whole social class, there are often common views about which emotions exist, which are the most valuable, which are to be avoided, and when and how to show them.

An emotional community will tend to have a shared mindset, embedded in a common emotional language. For instance, a community's restrained ethos might be conveyed by a tendency to describe tears and weeping with pejorative words like 'maudlin' or 'sentimental', rather than language that celebrated crying as a holy gift or a moral virtue. To take another example, we could think about the difference between sources describing sexual desires as 'sin' and 'lust' and those adopting a language of 'instinct' or 'natural feeling'. Emotions can neither fully develop nor be discussed with others without the medium of a shared language. As Rosenwein puts it:

> Because emotions are inchoate until they are given names, emotional vocabularies are exceptionally important for the ways in which people understand, express, and indeed 'feel' their emotions.

Emotional vocabularies come into use through the circulation, reception, discussion, and teaching of key texts within a community, whether those are works of scripture, drama, literature, psychology, popular music, or cinema. These provide the raw material for the emotional lexicon of a group, which over time must also establish rules about how those terms should be used. So, emotional communities are also verbal communities, held together by shared ways of speaking and writing about feelings.

Emotion words on their own may seem, in Carlyle's phrase, like 'so many Alphabetic Letters', and yet historians of emotions recognize that, by a curious and imperfect process of education and communal agreement, these groups of letters become not only the names of invisible feelings but also badges of membership and invitations to action. When children learn an emotion word like 'embarrassed' or 'gutted', they do not do so by consulting a dictionary, as they might with an abstract concept like 'biodiversity' or 'psychodynamic', nor by learning to name a simple sensation, as they might do for 'cold' or 'hungry'. They learn emotion words rather by repeated experiences of the social scenarios in which they hear them. They gradually learn that people say they are 'embarrassed' in situations where others see them in an unfavourable light, when they have done something wrong, perhaps when they are additionally feeling physically uncomfortable or are blushing, and are soliciting comfort or reassurance from others. History reinforces this realization: talking and writing about emotions is a way to manage and maintain social relationships.

Before 'the emotions'

An even more fundamental linguistic act that has shaped experiences of feeling over the centuries is categorizing them. To name and understand an experience as a 'feeling' or an 'emotion', rather than, say, a 'thought' or a 'sensation', is to put it in a particular place in our picture of our minds, bodies, and reality. For most of us that picture is somewhat hazy and not one we have necessarily spent a lot of time analysing. Nonetheless we indicate that we believe certain things about an experience by calling it an 'emotion'. This will not be the same as what someone else means by their use of the same word, and such differences of meaning have been all the more marked when we consider the changing connotations of the term, and numerous related categories, in English and other languages, through the ages.

In the most literal sense of the term, emotions are movements. 'Emotion' has its roots in the Latin verb *emovere* meaning to move out, displace, expel, or disturb. This was a verb of migration, commotion, and instability, originally in a physical sense. There are close equivalents in French, Spanish, and Italian, all of which have this shared sense of motion and agitation. In its earliest uses in English, from around the 1560s, 'emotions' could refer to civil disturbances or political conflicts, as in a report of 'The great tumultes and emotiones that were in Fraunce betwene the king and the nobilitie'. However 'emotion' was not a widely used term, and in 1603 Jean Florio, the translator into English of Michel de Montaigne's *Essais*, apologized to his readers for his introduction of various 'uncouth termes' from French into his translation, including 'emotion'. The historian encountering 'emotions' in early modern texts, then, needs to remember Febvre's warning against psychological anachronism and to understand the term as referring to 'commotions' or 'stirrings' in order to avoid projecting a modern sense of the word back into places where it does not belong.

Even when 'emotion' started to take on psychological meanings during the 17th and 18th centuries, these were different from the uses we are familiar with today. The French philosopher René Descartes made distinctive uses of the term *émotions* in his 1649 treatise on *The Passions of the Soul*, sometimes as an equivalent to *passions* and sometimes to refer to a narrow set of intellectual feelings. Several British philosophers used 'emotions' to mean the bodily signs of inward feelings, as when the founder of Utilitarianism, Jeremy Bentham, wrote in 1789: 'The emotions of the body are received, and with reason, as probable indications of the temperature of the mind.' Scottish philosophers of the 18th and 19th centuries, including David Hume and Dr Thomas Brown, were instrumental in introducing more modern uses of 'emotions' into academic discussions of the mind, and these were cemented by foundational texts of academic psychology, including works by Charles Darwin and William James, towards the end of the 19th century.

This history of the term 'emotion' is one reason why many historians would agree with the sentiment expressed by Penelope Gouk and Helen Hills in their introduction to an important 2005 collection of essays when they state that, 'Our starting-point is that "*the* emotions", unchanging within human nature, transcending historical conditions, do not exist.' So, if 'the emotions' do not exist in a universal way, were not a psychological category for most of human history, and continue not to be for many non-anglophone cultures, how else have love and hate, joy and sorrow, fear and rage been understood and categorized? There are as many answers to this as there are historical cultures, however the lack of an exact equivalent for 'the emotions' is a recurring theme. Neither the Bible, nor the Qu'rān, for instance, has a single category for emotion. They both deploy a range of categories and images, including ideas of 'hardness of heart' and 'thoughts of the heart', in which the heart is an organ of both thinking and feeling.

Two examples from different parts of the world, both developed around 2,500 years ago, can offer further insights: the idea of *qing* in Chinese philosophy and theories of 'the passions' as they developed from ancient Greek through to medieval and early modern thought. In modern Chinese thought, *qing* is often translated as 'emotions', alongside related terms such as *ganqing* meaning feeling or affection, and *qingxu* meaning mood. However *qing* did not always have this meaning. In ancient texts, *qing* referred to the facts of reality, and the genuine nature of things. In some philosophical texts produced during what is known as the Warring States period (475–221 BCE), the term's meaning changed, now referring to what we might call 'emotions' or 'dispositions' rather than to the facts of the physical world. It is unclear why this change occurred. Some have speculated that the emotions were considered what was most essential in human beings, and so the two uses are connected by this idea of a true essence. It is striking, whatever the reason for the change, that the same term could be transferred from physical nature to emotional states, suggesting the intimate connection between physical realities and the states of the mind that perceives those realities. The same semantic shift from physical to mental occurred, we may remember, with the English term 'emotions'.

Many important Chinese texts written in the same period still did not use the category of *qing*, despite having a focus on mental states that we might think of as emotions. The term does not appear, for instance, in the *Dao De Jing*, the founding text of the religion of Daoism, although the text is concerned with love, desire, anger, and compassion and their impact on behaviour and relationships. Similarly, in ancient Greece, early works of literature such as the epic poems ascribed to Homer, the *Iliad* and the *Odyssey*, are full of states of rage, desire, grief, and revenge, but the author and his contemporaries did not group these states together in a single category. *Pathē*, meaning 'the passions', emerged in Greek thought only around the 4th century BCE.

There are multiple reasons why *qing* and *pathē* are not the same things as 'the emotions', and should not be hastily translated into modern English-language psychological language. Two of those reasons concern what we might call the extension and the connotation of the words. In the philosophy of language, the 'extension' of a term is simply the set of things in the world that it applies to. The extension of 'table' is all tables, which of course then opens up the vexed but interesting question of which objects in the world count as tables, which need not detain us here. In the case of *qing*, we can look at the mental states that ancient Chinese thinkers included in its extension and compare those to the extension of the modern psychological category of 'emotions'. The result is a picture of two overlapping sets, something like a Venn diagram. Leaving aside for the moment the real problem of how accurately any ancient Chinese term can be rendered in modern English anyway, it seems that *qing* included states that could be translated as 'joy', 'anger', 'sadness', and 'fear', all of which appear on standard lists of basic emotions. However, *qing* could also include in its extension states of liking and disliking, love, pleasure, persuasion, reasoning, insolence, modesty, and the desire for material profit, which while very broadly emotional do not appear on standard lists of 'basic emotions'. On the other hand, some states enthusiastically studied as emotions by modern psychology, including 'disgust' and 'surprise', are not normally included under the category of *qing*.

To place a particular human experience into the category of *qing* or *pathē* was an evaluative and social act, and this is reflected in the historical connotations of those terms. In the western tradition of thought about *pathē*, or in Latin *passiones animae*—the passions of the soul—the dominant connotation was pathology (a term which shares its etymology with *pathē*). The passions were thought of as a moral and social problem to be wrestled with, often in a religious context. From ancient Greek philosophical texts onwards, the passions of the soul were variously characterized as diseases, intellectual mistakes, demonic desires, and dangerous wild animals. Especially in the realms of sex, violence, and the desire for material possessions, unregulated passions threatened to break the bonds of society and plunge individuals into brutal sin and eternal punishment. To name a state as a passion was to learn to experience it as a form of pathology—whether that pathology was medical or mental, moral or metaphysical.

Affects, atmospheres, and aliens

A powerful sense of pathology is one of the things that was lost in the transition from 'passions' to 'emotions' as the dominant modern category of feelings. For anyone learning about health and wellbeing today, whether in a classroom or via social media, the kind of message they are most likely to encounter is, 'Your emotions are valid and you are loved' or 'Your feelings are your feelings—they and you both deserve respect.' This sort of pro-emotion mantra is in stark contrast to the ideas of moralists and philosophers of the past who warned against the connections between passions, irrationality, and sinful behaviour. This has led some to suppose that in the past people believed that 'the emotions' were irrational, dangerous, and needed to be suppressed. However, again such a translation would be too hasty, because 'passions' and 'emotions' are not the same things.

Even the Stoics—rightly remembered as the philosophical school most hostile to the passions in all their forms—made use of an additional category of milder feelings called *eupatheiai*, which were what feelings could become when properly moderated and contained by reason. These modest feelings of joy, caution, and reasonable desire were allowable even for a Stoic. While the *eupatheiai* hardly sound like a lot of fun, they had a certain emotional quality. Within Christian teachings across the centuries, there were also ways to distinguish between virtuous and sinful mental states. 'Affections' of the soul that sprang from holy charity were quite different from vicious passions which revealed sinful earthly desires. The warnings of pre-modern thinkers against a particular set of passions should not, therefore, be mistaken for an expression of hostility towards the whole expansive modern category of 'the emotions'. Theories of the passions were complemented and supplemented with ideas about rational *eupatheiai* and godly 'affections'.

This brings us to the wide terrain of affects, affections, affectivity, and affect theory, which any historian of emotions will need to navigate. There are equivalent terms in many modern European languages, finding their roots in the Latin verb *afficere*, meaning to have an impact upon. Affects and affections, like passions, were originally passive states in which people felt they were being acted upon. In the history of philosophy, terms in this family have been used with quite specific meanings according to the system of their author. We have already seen that virtuous 'affections' could be contrasted with sinful passions by preachers and theologians. The Dutch Jewish philosopher Baruch Spinoza, in his posthumously published *Ethics* (1677), used this language in a different way, categorizing the modes of human thinking under three headings: *intellectus* (intellect), *conatus* (striving), and *affectus* (affects). The following century, the great Prussian philosopher Immanuel Kant developed his own threefold system, in which the mind had faculties of knowing, willing, and feeling. The faculty of feeling, or *Gefühl*, in turn was made up of several different kinds of desires and inclinations, including *Leidenschaften* and *Affekten*. None of Kant's terms maps straightforwardly on to a single English term such as 'passion', 'emotion', or 'affection'.

In modern psychology, 'affect' is an important term in two of the most influential, and mutually opposed, theoretical schools. The theory of hardwired 'basic emotions' was developed from an earlier theory of 'affect programs' proposed by the American psychologist Silvan Tomkins in the 1960s, which drew together approaches from evolutionary psychology and cybernetics. An 'affect program' is part computer program and part evolved instinct. If each of us has a mind like a Swiss army knife, which comes equipped with the same set of tools, then an affect program is one of those tools, with a distinctive physiological state and facial expression built in. The historian Ruth Leys has traced the history of this way of thinking about emotions in her critical study *The Ascent of Affect: Genealogy and Critique.* As Leys explains, theories of the kind favoured by Tomkins and Ekman treat affect programs, or basic emotions, as built-in reactions that can be triggered by environmental cues, but which do so without reference to questions of subjective meaning and interpretation.

The most influential alternative to the basic-emotions approach has been the theory of 'psychological construction', created and popularized since the 1990s by American psychologists James A. Russell and Lisa Feldman Barrett. Their way of thinking about and categorizing emotions makes a distinction between 'core affect', which is a deep, innate feeling system, and culturally specific 'emotions' which are constructed through the bringing together of core affect with the historically situated apparatus of language, thought, and experience. Core affect, on this theory, varies along two dimensions, namely valence and arousal. This means that an affective experience can be either pleasant or unpleasant (valence) and either high or low energy (arousal). This 'circumplex' model is a simple and powerful one which can be used to categorize emotions in a way that does not attempt to give universal status to particular modern English-language terms, such as 'fear', 'anger', and so on. This model has also been used to develop educational tools and even wellbeing apps, for instance through the work of the Yale Center for Emotional Intelligence and their RULER approach to emotional literacy.

The meaning of 'affect' takes on different connotations again within the cultural and social analyses representing the 'affective turn' of the last few decades. This turn can be traced back to multiple sources, including cultural studies, psychoanalytic thought, and continental philosophy. Influential contributors have included Raymond Williams, Eve Sedgwick, Gilles Deleuze, Brian Massumi, and Lauren Berlant. Each affect theorist has their own ideas about how to differentiate 'affect' from 'emotion', but they share an interest in going beyond the conscious, subjective meaning of an individual's emotions to find something more unconscious, impersonal, and collective. That something is 'affect'. Affect theorists try to bring to light the prelinguistic 'atmospheres', 'intensities', and 'structures of feeling' which make conscious personal emotions possible. The feminist historian and critic Sara Ahmed coined the term 'affect alien' to refer to social figures, such as the 'feminist killjoy' or the 'angry Black woman', whose resistance to repression is partly enacted by their resistance to prevailing structures of feeling.

One reason a thinker may refer to 'affect' rather than 'emotion' is to signal their allegiance to a particular intellectual and political position. From different standpoints, the category of 'emotions' can seem variously too scientific, too cognitive, too cerebral, too sentimental, too individualistic, too naive, or too secular. In those circumstances, 'affect' can be a useful alternative, as well as a badge of intellectual belonging. The very fact that historians and other scholars have become so interested in 'the emotions' in recent decades can make the category seem worn out, clichéd, or inimical to original thought.

A final reason that historians and others might prefer to write about the histories of 'affect' or 'experience' or 'sensibilities' rather than 'emotions' is to try to find a more neutral as well as a more original standpoint, detached from the implications of the modern psychological term 'emotions'. However there is no view from nowhere. Each term has its own theoretical baggage, and if it does not already, then it will do once it has been adopted by a particular group of scholars and writers. The appetite for intellectual innovation is healthy nonetheless, and the history of emotions itself is part of the endless but fascinating attempt to redefine key terms such as 'passion', 'feeling', or 'affect', showing once again how languages, theories, and experiences of emotion ebb and flow together over time.

Speaking without words

Our emotional states can be represented and conveyed through non-verbal languages, as well as with words. Thinking back to Adele's tearful apology on Instagram, for instance, that was a multimodal, multimedia, emotional performance. Feeling was conveyed not just through the singer's words, but also through her body language, her hand movements, her breathing, her tone of voice, from distraught and plaintive to fragile and tremulous, and through her various facial expressions. To call this a performance is not to suggest it was insincere. Emotions are frequently social

From passions to emojis

performances, involving multiple learned non-verbal elements, whether the state of feeling is authentically represented by them or not. Indeed, we may not even know for sure ourselves whether our performances are wholly authentic or if we have perhaps unconsciously hammed things up a bit for our audience of loved ones or colleagues.

The theory that there is a bodily and facial language of human expression—that the emotions of the body are probable indications of the temperature of the mind, as Bentham put it—may be universal across cultures. What is not universal, however, is the vocabulary and grammar found in such languages. Both the ancient Indian aesthetic theory of *rasa* and modern theories of affect programs or basic emotions, for instance, offer ways to read the emotional human body, including rather exaggerated and formalized facial expressions. However, the details vary significantly.

One of the foundational texts of *rasa* theory is a Sanskrit text called the Nāṭya Śāstra, or the *Treatise on Drama*, written in the early centuries CE. The text identifies a list of various *rasas*, which are what we might call the emotional tone or flavour of a particular work of art or moment of performance. *Rasa* literally means 'juice' or 'essence', and so the *rasa* is the emotional flavour of a scene. Even leaving aside the hugely different cultural practices motivating the theories of *rasa* and basic emotions, respectively, a superficial examination of the faces, taken by some western observers to represent particular emotions, demonstrates how the traditions diverge. For instance, the facial expressions associated with the *raudra rasa*, the *rasa* generally thought to be closest to western 'anger', look more like the faces associated by modern psychologists with 'surprise' or 'disgust' (see Figure 5).

Rich representations of the passions of the soul are to be found in the histories of visual art, morality, and religion in medieval and early modern Europe. Many of these images had an explicitly

5. The *raudra rasa* is sometimes described as corresponding to the western emotion of 'anger', although the expression seems closer to those associated with surprise or disgust by basic-emotion theorists.

didactic purpose, showing their viewers what their feelings might look like, which cases of godly affection or holy tears they should emulate, and which sensual desires and passions most urgently to resist. One such illustration was added as a frontispiece to the English translation of a work on *The Use of the Passions*, originally published in French in 1641 by the Catholic philosopher Jean-François Senault. This engraving summarizes the teaching of the book in visual form, showing the passions of the soul chained together like prisoners, and being brought before the figures of reason and divine grace to account for themselves (Figure 6).

In a way we could see an image like this as a forerunner of the modern psychological attempt to link particular emotion words with particular expressions, even though the list of passions here differs from standard lists of 'basic emotions'. However there are further reasons, in the complex symbolism, the inclusion of bodily gestures and props, and the implied moral narratives, to maintain a sense of the distance between this illustration and the modern

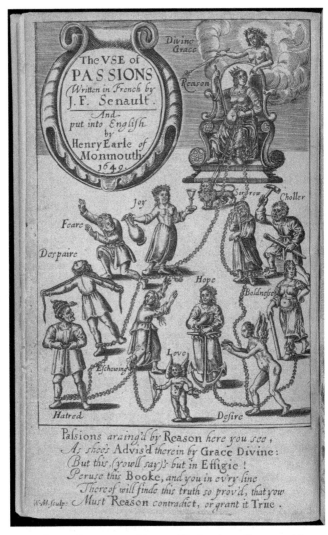

6. The frontispiece to Senault's *Use of the Passions* offers a graphic illustration of Christian ideas about the relationship between divine grace, reason, and the passions.

psychological project. The picture contains representations of rebellion, violence, and slavery which had very particular meanings in the 17th century, in both theological and political contexts, including the idea that sinful human beings are slaves held in bondage by their passions. It also hints at the explicitly royalist message of the English version of the text, which was published in 1649, the same year that Charles I had been beheaded: if you wish to govern others you must be able to govern your own passions.

The most recent additions to the panoply of languages of emotion are emoticons and emojis. There are examples of playful uses of typographical features to represent facial expressions of feeling in the 19th century, such as a whimsical *Studies in Passions and Emotions* created by the American satirical magazine *Puck* in 1881 (Figure 7). Claims have been made for earlier examples of similar practices, even going back to the 17th century. However emoticons only started to be used more widely to express positive or negative emotional reactions from the 1980s onwards, and their cousins the pictographic emojis made their first appearances on Japanese mobile phones in the late 1990s. Emojis are now a near-universal feature of communication on smartphones and social media. They include representations of simple angry, tearful, or laughing faces, and much more besides, including faces with eyes replaced by hearts or stars, vomiting faces, thumbs up or down, shrugging shoulders, a face based on the Munch painting *The Scream*, crossed fingers, waving hands, upside-down faces, sleeping faces, skulls, aliens, animals, excrement, foods, drinks, sporting equipment, teddy bears, nail scissors, and toilet rolls.

There are thousands of emojis, some more emotional than others. As with Adele's addition of a red broken-heart emoji to her apologetic social media post, we can now either replace or supplement our words from this huge range of symbols and pictograms which act as a kind of emotional seasoning, adding a

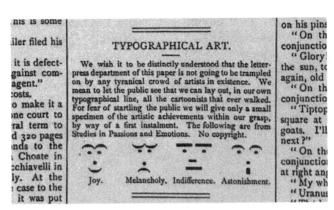

7. **Early experiments with using typographical features to create emotional expressions include this short article in *Puck* magazine in 1881.**

feeling flavour to a textual or visual message. And, as in past centuries, the visual and the verbal continue to inform and shape each other. Every year the Oxford Dictionaries announce their 'Word of the Year'. In 2015, for the first and only time so far the 'word' of the year was not a word in the usual sense but instead the 'Face With Tears of Joy' emoji. This was the most used emoji globally in 2015, and was taken by Oxford Dictionaries to best represent the 'ethos, mood, and preoccupations' of the year, including the massively increased use both of emojis and of the word 'emoji'.

I have encountered in my own work with schools in England evidence of the ways that the boundaries can be blurred between emojis and emotion words. In one exercise, I ask children simply to list as many different emotions as they can think of. I have noticed names of emojis such as 'meh' and 'winky' making their way on to these lists. Some cultural commentators express concern about this kind of emojification. They fear that children communicating with each other via smartphones and social media, using text speak and emojis rather than formal language, have an impoverished vocabulary. However, it could be instead that the advent of emojis in the early 21st century simply represents the next stage in millennia of cultural history, in which words, images, and emotions continue to change and evolve together.

Chapter 4
Terror and the pursuit of happiness

It is not unusual to hear parents saying about their children, 'All I really want is for them to be happy', as if happiness might be relatively easily achieved compared to, say, academic success, a lucrative career, or international fame and glory. We may not be sure precisely what people mean when they say this, but the dominant modern idea of 'happiness' is an emotional one—it is about feeling good more often than not. Modern happiness is sometimes thought of as a kind of 'subjective wellbeing', in which pleasures outnumber pains, desires are satisfied, and special moments are enjoyed to the full. A happy life, in this sense, is one full of positive emotions.

The shadow side of a parent's hope that their child will be happy is the fear that they will not. Polls suggest parents are indeed full of fears and anxieties on behalf of their offspring. They worry about their children's educational development being harmed by the impact of Covid; about social media and cyberbullying; about racism, climate change, violence, and poverty; and about all these things making their children depressed, stressed, and anxious. When it comes to our own emotions and those of our loved ones it sometimes seems that, to use a phrase made famous by President Franklin D. Roosevelt in his 1933 inaugural address, 'the only thing we have to fear is fear itself'.

A dual focus on happiness and anxiety is also evident in the way that modern governments measure and think about the emotional lives of their citizens. In the United Kingdom, four questions about feelings are asked by the Office for National Statistics as part of their Annual Population Survey. The first two ask how satisfied people are with their lives in general, and whether they feel the things they do are worthwhile. The next two are about more transitory emotions: 'How happy did you feel yesterday?' and 'How anxious did you feel yesterday?' Participants are directed to answer each question by choosing a number from 0 to 10 to represent their feelings. Through this simple technique, the apparently intangible emotional state of a nation can be made into a numerical, graphable, crunchable reality. We can plot the peaks and troughs of national mood as the years pass, charting our levels of happiness and fear through financial crises, political upheavals, and global pandemics.

Collective emotions and statistics can enter into a vicious circle, as people feel increasingly worried about studies showing increasing levels of anxiety, which in turn is reflected in their answers to questions about how anxious they felt yesterday. Living under a government that is actively trying to maximize happiness and minimize anxiety might not be a recipe for, well, happiness. The pressure of expectation on our children to achieve and display happiness throughout their lives might also be a source of anxiety rather than happiness, and some fear that messages delivered by schools and charities promoting resilience, mindfulness, a growth mindset, and positive thinking amount to a kind of 'toxic positivity'.

This modern to-and-fro between happiness, anxiety, and the state can be identified as a 'structure of feeling'—a recurring pattern of emotions made possible by social and cultural factors. We can trace its origins back to the politics and culture of the 18th century, when emotions and politics were starting to take on their modern shape. The 18th-century pursuit of happiness brought with it new terrors and anxieties. Happiness was a foundational aim for revolutionaries in both North America and France. It was written into the Declaration of Independence of the United States of America in 1776, and echoed in the Declaration of the Rights of Man adopted by France's new National Assembly in 1789. The shadow side of this aspiration was evident in the violence and bloodshed of the armed revolutions undertaken in its name. The waves of revolutionary ecstasy had an undertow of terror, and the pursuit of happiness was haunted by fear.

The emotional pairing analysed in this chapter is useful for our purposes for another reason, too. The era in which this particular configuration of happiness and terror emerged was one that has been of special interest to historians of emotions more broadly. The 18th century saw the birth of what historians have termed a new 'culture of sensibility', in which educated ladies and gentlemen displayed their moral refinement and human sympathy by responding emotionally to sentimental plays, novels, and paintings. This culture was one in which sympathy for one's fellow men and women, and public expressions of certain emotions, were newly valued alongside the powers of reason and intellect. Eighteenth-century sensibility found expression in religion and politics as well as in the art and literature of the age. Among the emotions most celebrated were love, compassion, and ecstasy as well as a delightful kind of aesthetic terror known as the 'sublime'.

An idea shared by many who adopted both the philosophy of sensibility and the ideals of the American and French Revolutions was that there was something universal about human nature, and that certain 'rights' flowed from that. All human beings had powers of reason, were linked by their powers of sympathetic feeling, and were owed dignity, liberty, and the protection of the state. The universality of this theory of rights and feelings, however, was not matched in practice. Whether understood as a political aspiration or as an emotional experience, 'happiness' was never equally available to all. There were many, including women and people of colour, who were forced to smile through their suffering in a show of cheerful submission, masking emotions of pain, despair, and terror, while being offered little of the sympathy and compassion lauded by the era's moralists.

What was happiness in 1776?

In the 18th century, as today, people could mean different things when they talked about 'happiness'. The ancestry of the idea of happiness as an emotional state that can be measured numerically in wellbeing surveys is to be found in the figure of the English thinker and social reformer Jeremy Bentham, founder of the philosophy of Utilitarianism. His key idea was that the aim of all individual actions and government policies should be to secure 'the greatest happiness of the greatest number'. Bentham thought of this 'happiness' in both an emotional and a mathematical way. It was the surplus of pleasures over pains and, in theory at least, those states of feeling could be quantified and measured.

Bentham's philosophy gained more supporters during the 19th century but his was not the most influential understanding of happiness in the era of the American and French Revolutions. To find that we need to look instead at the Declaration of Independence adopted by the 13 original 'united States of America' at the Second Continental Congress in Philadelphia on 4 July 1776. The document was drafted by Thomas Jefferson and edited by a committee whose members included John Adams and Benjamin Franklin. After a preliminary opening sentence about the need to break the historic bonds between one people and another, the text famously proceeds:

> We hold these truths to be self-evident, that all men are created equal, that they are endowed by their Creator with certain unalienable Rights, that among these are Life, Liberty and the pursuit of Happiness.

The declaration goes on to affirm the intention of the people of the newly independent states to form for themselves a government on such principles that 'shall seem most likely to effect their Safety and Happiness'.

Happiness, then, was a central ideal for the newly founded United States of America. But what kind of 'happiness' did Jefferson and his colleagues have in mind? It was something quite different from Bentham's measurable state of feeling, and it had its roots in older, non-emotional meanings of the term. The 'hap' in 'happiness' is the same as the 'hap' in 'perhaps' and 'happenstance'. In other words, it refers to luck, or chance, rather than to emotions. In some contexts, that meaning is still preserved, as when we refer to a 'happy coincidence'. To be happy in this sense is to be lucky, to enjoy good fortune. Among the other non-emotional uses of 'happiness' is the way it has been defined in philosophical and political contexts to refer to the broadest aims of human life. 'Happiness' is sometimes used, for instance, to translate the ancient Greek *eudaimonia*, a term for human flourishing. To achieve *eudaimonia* was to live successfully, which, for Aristotle and others, meant living in accordance with virtue and reason.

The kind of 'happiness' that the founders of the United States had in mind was within this non-emotional group of meanings. One clue pointing towards this interpretation is a short essay, 'On True Happiness', written by Benjamin Franklin and published in the *Pennsylvania Gazette* some decades earlier. In that essay Franklin made a distinction between two possible kinds of happiness. The first was sensual and passionate, a state achieved by following one's most immediate sensory appetites. This was a recipe, the essay argued, for a life of mental disquiet, unquenchable desires, envy, and disappointment. Franklin contrasted this sorry state with 'true, solid happiness', which was grounded in 'an indifference to the things of this world, an entire submission to the will of Providence here, and a well-grounded expectation of happiness hereafter'. For Franklin and those who thought like him, the pursuit of happiness was mainly about being good rather than feeling good. When they inscribed the pursuit of 'happiness' into their nation's founding document, what they dreamed of was a country where people could live in freedom, virtue, and prosperity, but not necessarily one where everybody felt cheerful or tried to maximize their positive emotions. Those aspirations would come later. 'Happiness' in 1776 was the ability to pursue prosperity through the solid and sober exercise of reason and virtue.

The most frantic joy

While modern 'happiness' may be too emotional a concept to help us understand the earnest ideals of the founders of the United States, it is not emotional enough to capture the experience of the early days of the French Revolution. One first-hand account recorded the ecstatic atmosphere after the storming of the Bastille on 14 July 1789:

> A sudden burst of the most frantic joy instantaneously took place; every possible mode in which the most rapturous feelings of joy could be expressed, were everywhere exhibited. Shouts and shrieks, leaping and embracing, laughter and tears, every sound and every gesture, including even what approached to nervous and hysterical affection, manifested among the promiscuous crowd.

This author concluded that he had just witnessed 'such an instantaneous and unanimous emotion of extreme gladness as I should suppose was never before experienced by human beings'. As an aside, we should note that 'emotion' is used here in its pre-psychological sense, to mean an outward expression or agitation. Other accounts of the same event similarly recalled tears of joy and cries of jubilation on this occasion, and at other key moments, such as the Festival of Federation in the summer of 1790, held to mark the revolution's first anniversary. Families celebrated together, old men knelt and gave thanks that they had seen this joyful dawn, tearful mothers vowed to teach their infants the principles of *liberté, egalité*, and *fraternité*. It was a moment of contagious enthusiasm and thrilling political sentiment.

Looking back at the early days of the French Revolution later in life, the Romantic poet William Wordsworth recalled this ecstatic atmosphere. 'Bliss was it in that dawn to be alive,' he wrote, 'But to be young was very heaven!' Here was a country caught up in the romance of its own unfolding history. Wordsworth's poem was published in 1809 under the title 'The French Revolution, As It Appeared to Enthusiasts at Its Commencement'. Another English writer, Helen Maria Williams, had published a series of *Letters Written in France*. Reporting on the Festival of Federation in the summer of 1790, she described her response to the collective jubilation: 'my heart caught with enthusiasm the general sympathy; my eyes were filled with tears; and I shall never forget the sensations of that day'. In a later letter, Williams sounded a more cautious note, contrasting French sensibilities with the emotional style of her home country: 'We seem to have a strange dread in England of indulging any kind of enthusiasm.'

Today, 'enthusiasm' is a term for keen interest, perhaps even passionate commitment, but it is a relatively tame concept compared to its meanings in the 17th and 18th centuries. Then it referred to the most fervent feelings of bliss, joy, and ecstasy. It was an emotional style associated with religious groups, especially those sometimes called the 'hotter sort of Protestant', who enjoyed dramatic preaching and emotional hymns, as well as weeping, shouting, shaking, falling down, and speaking in tongues. This kind of enthusiasm was a hallmark of the Anabaptist sect in Germany in the 16th century, of Quakers and Shakers in 17th-century England, whose very names reflected their bodily practices, as well as of Pietist denominations in Europe, and subsequently of the Methodist movement.

Methodism started within the Church of England in the 18th century, and became an independent Protestant grouping with huge influence in Britain, the United States, and beyond. Accounts of Methodist lives preserved in the historical record tend to follow the same, highly emotional pattern. A potent awareness of sin, accompanied by feelings of self-loathing and tears of agony, is succeeded by a moment of ecstatic revelation of the love of Jesus, accompanied by tears of joy and shouts of jubilation. A satirical image from the 1760s by William Hogarth originally entitled 'Enthusiasm Delineated' portrayed a Methodist congregation being whipped into a frantic state by their preacher, while indulging in deranged and immoral acts (Figure 8). In the corner of the print is a barometer measuring the spiritual temperature. The emotional scale rises from agony, sorrow, and despair, via lusts, convulsions, and madness, to divine joy and ecstasy. Enthusiasm, in this picture, is a deluded and overheated form of madness. To some, the French Revolution seemed a manifestation of enthusiasm of a similar kind.

Enthusiasm has continued to be an important topic in the sociology, anthropology, and history of emotions. Collective joy, ecstasy, and even delirium have been experienced historically in the worlds not only of religion and politics but also of sports, entertainment, and social rites of passage. The sociologist Émile Durkheim referred to acts of 'collective effervescence' that are learned and reproduced through social rituals. The anthropologist and historian Monique Scheer has also explored the history of enthusiasm as an emotional practice that has been performed in a range of religious settings in Germany since the 19th century. Scheer has been a pioneer of an approach which treats emotions as bodily practices—things that people do, rather than merely feel. Her historical research and fieldwork in modern religious life proceeds on the understanding that all emotional styles have their own distinctive material and social conditions:

CREDULITY, SUPERSTITION, and FANATICISM.
A MEDLEY.
Believe not every Spirit but try the Spirits whether they are of God: because many false Prophets are gone out into the World. 1 John Ch 4 V 1.
Design'd and Engrav'd by Wᵐ Hogarth.   Published as the Act directs March ᵍ 15ᵗʰ 1762.

8. William Hogarth satirized the extreme religious emotions of the Methodists in the 18th century in this print, originally entitled 'Enthusiasm Delineated'.

Not just the colorful imagery of Latin American Catholicism or Tibetan Buddhism, but also the stark white-washed walls of Calvinist interiors mediate the supernatural, the whirling of Sufi dance as well as the quiet concentration of Zen meditation.

A shared architecture, atmosphere, and set of rules about expression create the conditions for collective emotions such as religious enthusiasm. However, there is a continuing relationship between an individual's behaviour and the collective, rather than a complete dissolution of one within the other. Not everyone at the funeral weeps. Not everyone at the football match joins in with the chants. Not everyone gives the orchestra a standing ovation. Not everyone has a conversion experience. And someone who felt ecstatic bliss at an event in their youth may later view it as a moment of dangerous enthusiasm as they grow older or move from one emotional community into another. The history of emotions is a story of individuals in constant dynamic interaction with the social structures around them.

The first terrorists

The perception of a new dawn in 1789 had led many to join in with a collective enthusiasm; however it was not long before that feeling was joined by a rising terror. Before the French Revolution, 'terror' had a range of connotations, some of them quite positive. God, or strong earthly rulers, could inspire a terror which was a mixture of fear, reverence, and respect. Punishments for crimes were thought to inspire a fitting terror in potential miscreants. Sublime terror was an awe-struck astonishment in the face of a spectacle of power and beauty, whether a work of art or of nature—an overwhelming oil-painting or a thrillingly dangerous avalanche. In his *Philosophical Enquiry into the Origin of Our Ideas of the Sublime and the Beautiful* (1757), the Irish thinker Edmund Burke suggested that this kind of exquisite aesthetic feeling arose 'when we have an idea of pain and danger, without being actually in such circumstances'. This was the 'strongest emotion which the mind is capable of feeling', Burke wrote, and anything that gave rise to this delightful terror was what he meant by the 'sublime'.

'Terror' took on a new meaning during the 1790s primarily as the result of the career of Maximilien Robespierre—the bespectacled and fastidious provincial lawyer who became the architect of the most bloody and authoritarian period of the French Revolution, known as the Reign of Terror, from September 1793 to July 1794. In Robespierre's own political vision, happiness and terror were both important, and indeed they were combined in an idea of zealous revolutionary feeling which sounded a lot like Burke's idea of the delightful terror of the sublime. Robespierre claimed that his revolutionary government would replace the sensual self-indulgence of the old aristocratic regime with merit, truth, virtue, and 'the charm of happiness', creating 'a people who are magnanimous, powerful, and happy'. Robespierre saw no contradiction in stating that his policy was 'to lead the people by reason and the people's enemies by terror', explaining that this 'terror' was the 'prompt, severe, inflexible justice' needed to protect the new constitution, and usher in the longed-for age of happiness.

However joyful its public celebrations, the revolution was, of course, always a terrifyingly violent event, even before the rise of Robespierre. The rapturous gladness of the crowd after the fall of the Bastille was a response to an event in which the prison governor's head was cut off by an armed mob and carried through the streets of Paris on a spike. *Fraternité* had its limits when it came to the old regime, and the new world order was swept in on a tide of death and bloodshed. Thousands would be summarily dispatched by the guillotine or by lawless acts of political murder. Perhaps that is why, even in the earliest accounts of the revolution, there is the sense of a frightening hysteria beneath the bliss and hope of the moment. Such frantic joy is not a stable basis for anything.

The historian Timothy Tackett has made a detailed study of the emotional dynamics at play during the Terror. He argues that the enthusiasm of the early revolutionaries—their bliss at the new dawn—was fuelled by hope for a genuinely novel form of government, rather than by vengeance or hatred. However,

Tackett goes on, 'from the very beginning, the powerful emotions of joy and enthusiasm engendered by the Revolution's extraordinary achievements were mixed with feelings of anxiety'. That anxiety grew rapidly in scope and power, until it reached the fully fledged paranoia of the Terror. Suspicion, rumour, delusion, and panic mixed with instances of genuine betrayal and disloyalty, to create an atmosphere in which the purported rationality, brotherhood, and happiness of the revolution could be entirely drowned by fear.

When Robespierre himself was executed by guillotine in July 1794, screaming in agony from an injury sustained during his arrest, the crowd erupted in joyous celebration, happy to see the painful death of the author of their fears. So the emotional cycle of terror and happiness continued. After Robespierre's death, people were keen to distance themselves from his regime. One way they did so was through a new pejorative language of 'terrorism'. The idea took hold that Robespierre had presided over a 'system of terror' and that his methods represented something called 'terrorism'. In 1795 Edmund Burke was an early user of this terminology when he wrote that 'Thousands of those hell-hounds called terrorists were let loose on the people.' During the 19th century 'terrorism' became the name for a campaign of violence against both military and civilian targets aimed at coercing a government into a change of policy. This meaning is now the dominant one, so that what started as a word for an authoritarian government has become a term for non-governmental groups using terrifying and deadly violence in pursuit of their aims.

A phobic regime

The French clergyman Nicolas Coeffeteau, in his 1620 *Table of Human Passions*, had stated that fear (in French he used both *la peur* and *la crainte*) was a response to the thought of a future calamity, and was always 'accompanied with a certain horror which amazes the senses'. In other words, a full-blown fearful passion only existed when the body was also involved. Coeffeteau listed a pale complexion, rapidly beating heart, and trembling limbs among the passion's effects. Two and a half centuries later, Charles Darwin went a step further in suggesting that emotions were almost identical with their physical expressions. He recalled an anecdote about an unemotional Louis XVI who, when surrounded by an angry mob during the revolution, exclaimed, 'Am I afraid? Feel my pulse.' For early modern theologians and defiant French kings, as for modern psychologists, if there was no bodily arousal, there was no fear.

Modern technology and psychiatry have reshaped the range and nature of fearful experiences during the last two centuries. While fear, terror, worry, anxiety, and phobias are all related emotions, they are by no means identical with each other, and the most common objects of these feelings have changed over time too. In earlier eras, men and women trembled in fear at the thought of destitution, disease, death, and divine judgement. The rise of modernity ushered in a different world where the most pressing fears were man-made. Hell on earth became an even more terrifying, and more likely, prospect than eternal punishment at the hands of the devil. Historians of emotions have shown how the changing nature of both warfare and medical practice modernized fearful feelings, while evolutionary psychology and psychoanalysis shaped the lexicon available to people to describe their emotions, and heralded the dawn of a new 'phobic regime'.

Jan Plamper has researched the emotional responses of Russian soldiers in the early 20th century. Fear and terror were increasingly common responses to the new and extreme psychological stresses of modern warfare, which involved facing rifle and machine-gun fire and aerial bombardment while confined within a system of trench-warfare. Plamper also discusses the creation of new literary genres offering greater realism about the horrors of war, starting with Leo Tolstoy's 1855 *Sevastopol Sketches*, which drew on the author's experiences of warfare, including a near-fatal shell attack, to conjure up the terrifying realities faced by soldiers, and their emotional impacts. These trends helped to produce a culture in the early 20th century that allowed for public discussions of the mental effects of war, in Russia and beyond, drawing on new medical diagnoses with names such as 'military contusion', 'traumatic neurosis', 'male hysteria', and 'shell shock'.

We can discern similar trends towards newly medicalized languages of fear in Europe and America. Joanna Bourke has documented a shift in the language used by servicemen to describe their emotions, from an evolutionary vocabulary of 'animal instinct' and 'primitive blood-lust' in the first half of the 20th century to more Freudian self-reports after the Second World War, as in the case of an American soldier who described fear in combat producing 'an ache as profound as the ache of orgasm'. Bourke also looks at the topic of religious fears in the light of this rise in psychoanalytic models. A mid-20th-century survey of Catholic high-school pupils in the state of New York asked about their experience of religious 'scruples'. This meant how often they worried about things such as resisting temptations, confessing their sins, or performing due penance. To have fears about such failings and their consequences was a sign of piety within the religious context, but according to 20th-century psychiatry it indicated 'psychasthenia', 'anxiety disorder', or 'obsessive-compulsive disorder'. Under this modern 'phobic regime' moral and religious frameworks for fear were replaced by medical ones. 'Agoraphobia' and 'claustrophobia' were both coined in the 1870s, for instance, and 'arachnophobia' in the 1920s. 'School phobia' was proposed in the 1940s as a new, respectable medical name for a condition afflicting middle-class children who would not attend school.

The idea that those who enjoyed extreme sports like white-water rafting, parachuting, or bungee jumping were 'adrenaline junkies' in search of their next 'adrenaline rush' originated in North

America in the 1970s and spread round the world from there, reflecting again the increasing influence of physiological ways of thinking and talking about emotions. The popularity of such activities testified also to the continuing connection between terror and enjoyment in the modern world, as did the continuing demand for horror movies, which had been providing a safe social setting in which to enjoy the delightful pains of fictional terror since the 1890s.

If you just smile

We can connect these strands of the histories of happiness and terror, ecstasy and anxiety, together by observing that it was not just political, but also emotional regimes which underwent a revolution during the 18th century. The historian of medicine and emotions Colin Jones has also made this point, in his account of the 'smile revolution' that took place at that time in Paris, overturning a previous emotional order under which showing the teeth in a smile was thought coarse, impolite, or even bestial. That started to change in the second half of the century, thanks to a combination of improved dentistry and the new culture of sensibility. By the time of the revolution such open-mouthed smiles were highly fashionable and became visible in both portraits and public life as signs of sweetness and humanity. During the Terror, a smile could also be a sign of defiance. The king's sister was one of many who were seen to smile serenely through their trial and execution. Another was the intellectual and writer Madame Roland, who delivered her famous final words with a bitter smile on her lips: 'Oh liberty! What crimes are committed in your name!'

In more recent decades others have similarly embraced joy as a gesture of political defiance. In her 1970 bestseller *The Female Eunuch* the feminist writer Germaine Greer wrote that 'the struggle that is not joyous is the wrong struggle'. This joy, for Greer, was not a kind of 'hedonism and hilarity', but rather a feeling of purpose and dignity, 'which is the reflowering of etiolated energy'. In the 21st century, the non-violent Extinction Rebellion protest movement has an ethos of protest characterized by 'joy, creativity and beauty' in the face of the climate crisis. Others have advocated 'Black joy' as an act of resistance in a white-supremacist world.

Historically, though, outward smiles and cheerfulness often masked oppression. Patriarchal husbands, draconian employers, and slaveholders demanded visible signs of cheer in their wives, workers, and slaves. In *A Vindication of the Rights of Woman* (1792), the English political philosopher Mary Wollstonecraft described smiling as one of the characteristics of the submissive and servile ideal of womanhood that dominated her culture. Too many women were taught to have ambitions that went no further than pleasing their husbands with their beauty and adornments, with femininity and forbearance. Wollstonecraft argued that women should not be duped by an idealization of a feminized figure of 'gentleness' which in reality was a poor and submissive creature 'smiling under the lash at which it dare not snarl'.

The emotions of African American slaves were also a site of political domination and exploitation. As Nicole Eustace has discovered, slaveholders rarely commented on the emotions of their slaves in the 18th century, other than occasionally to talk about their dull and downcast demeanour. This was connected with one of the attempted justifications of slavery: that some types of people were 'natural slaves' with limited capacity for any kind of feelings. A different argument became more common in the 19th century, namely that slaves did have the capacity for human feelings, but that they were generally very happy with their lot. This was the standard line among pro-slavery writers in the era of the Civil War. The Governor of South Carolina claimed that there was 'not a happier, more contented race upon the face of the earth than our slaves'. However, as the testimonies of former slaves revealed, any superficial appearance of good cheer was produced, like their labour, by force. Slaves who failed to display a sunny disposition by smiling, laughing, and singing, would be whipped or sold.

In 20th- and 21st-century economies where service industries dominate, forced emotional displays took on a new aspect, in the creation of roles where such performances were a central part of the job itself. In her influential 1983 work *The Managed Heart*, the American sociologist Arlie Russell Hochschild coined the term 'emotional labor' to refer to the act of producing a public display of feeling in return for wages. She spent time with trainee flight attendants and saw how they were taught to think of their smile as an 'asset' to exploit to make customers feel good about their experience of flying. But, as in method acting, the smile had to appear genuine rather than just painted on. The attendants and their passengers had to feel the smile. One woman newly qualified in the role described her emotional exhaustion after a long trip: 'I can't relax. I giggle a lot, I chatter, I call friends. It's as if I can't release myself from an artificially created elation that kept me "up" on the trip.' Hochschild suggested that in emotional labour, people are alienated from their own emotions.

Nineteenth-century working-class autobiographies offer glimpses of emotional labour in the past, such as the strolling performer whose work was to entertain theatre crowds with an act including monkey impressions, but who wrote that the audience could not see 'the bitterness of spirit that is hidden under the grinning mask and grotesque antics of the miserable clown who excites their thoughtless laughter'. A young woman who worked in a factory in Glasgow, and had been abused for years by her stepfather, recalled how she learned to conceal her sorrows: 'I often smiled when my heart was weeping—the gilded mask of false merriment made me often appear happy in company.' Those who had sustained severe injuries through industrial accidents or in military service, people with disabilities, and men and women facing the infirmities of old age were all encouraged to bear their difficulties with cheerfulness.

Women have been expected to perform positive emotions in many contexts. When a bride is told her wedding will be the 'happiest day of her life', that can function as a demand to perform happiness for the benefit of others, rather than a promise of true joy for the bride herself. Historical accounts survive of the painful contrast between that particular expectation and reality. A young woman who married in rural northern Italy in 1950 recalled that although on her wedding day she seemed outwardly happy, she was filled with terror and despair thinking of what lay ahead of her, moving in with her husband's family after the wedding, as was customary. 'Even though I very much loved the man I was marrying,' she wrote, 'to me it seemed it was the day of my hanging.' Her horror of what lay ahead manifested itself physically, too: 'I saw everything double, I had a splitting headache. I didn't say anything to anyone.'

In the modern world, men still shout 'Smile, love!' at women they do not know, and tell them they would look more attractive smiling. There remains, then, good reason to echo Wollstonecraft's argument that women need to be freed from the expectation of simpering man-pleasing. In her 1970 book *The Dialectic of Sex: The Case for Feminist Revolution*, Shulamith Firestone wrote about how she had trained herself out of 'that phony smile, which is like a nervous tic on every teenage girl', and said that her dream action for the women's liberation movement would be a smile boycott in which 'all women would instantly abandon their "pleasing" smiles, henceforth smiling only when something pleased them'. Sara Ahmed has built on these ideas, combining the history of emotions, affect theory, and feminist politics in books including her *Promise of Happiness* (2010), and its chapter on 'Feminist Killjoys'. Since 2012 the American artist Tatyana Fazlalizadeh has been producing public art to address street

9. Tatyana Fazlalizadeh's street-art project 'Stop telling women to smile' addresses gender-based street harassment, and began in Brooklyn in 2012.

harassment of women through a project called 'Stop Telling Women to Smile' (Figure 9).

On wedding days, in unhappy families, in slavery, in paid work, and on the streets, women and men have historically had to mask their emotional misery and fear behind a forced smile. This realization puts our world of smiley faces, happiness surveys, and employee wellbeing programmes in a different light. Smiles, grins, and grimaces can convey aggression, pain, or terror, as well as either genuine or apparent happiness. The coerced smile is the subject of a haunting artwork by the Ghanaian-born British artist Harold Offeh. His 2001 video piece, entitled simply 'Smile', was inspired by the song of that title written by Charlie Chaplin, encouraging the listener to smile through their fears and sorrows. 'Smile' comprises just under three minutes of a tight close-up of Offeh's face, as he smiles and grimaces to the accompaniment of Nat King Cole's 1954 rendition of the song (see Figure 10). As the strings soar, Offeh's eyes open wide and his cheek muscles work to

10. **Harold Offeh's 2001 piece of video art 'Smile' offers an uncomfortable reflection on the history of forced cheerfulness.**

reveal his clenched teeth trying to maintain a grin. As one critic put it, the work is 'arresting and gently upsetting'. As Nat King Cole's mellifluous voice assures us that 'You'll find that life is still worthwhile, if you just smile', we might hear the echo of another bold assertion from the past—'there is not a happier, more contented race upon the face of the earth than our slaves'.

Chapter 5
All the rages

Anger was one of the first topics to receive sustained attention in the early years of the history of emotions as an emerging field of study. *Anger: The Struggle for Emotional Control in America's History* by Carol and Peter Stearns was published in 1986. This pioneering foray into irate history interpreted its subject as a biologically inscribed 'fight' response, somewhat along the lines of the basic-emotions theory. Although Stearns and Stearns disavowed any attempt to define 'anger' explicitly, the way they wrote suggested a belief in a single underlying, instinctual emotion, which American society had accommodated or resisted within the domains of marriage, child-rearing, and work, in various ways.

'Anger' is indeed one of the most frequently cited contenders for the status of a universal emotion. It features on every major list of 'basic emotions' produced by psychologists who believe in such things, and so is an especially interesting and challenging subject for the history of emotions, which, as a general approach, has tended to take the inadequacy of the 'basic emotions' theory as one of its starting points. This chapter takes on that challenge by seeking out the differences between various historical states of ire, wrath, rage, and revenge, which might, at first glance, seem to be examples of a singular emotion of 'anger'. Changing ideas about vengeance, violence, sin, and aggression have made different ideas and experiences of ire and irritation available across the centuries, which differ both from each other and from modern notions of 'anger'.

Research by historians of emotions in recent years has shown how many different feelings and behaviours have been associated with 'anger', 'rage', and related terms, including, but not restricted to: the desire for revenge, whether human or demonic, a hardwired brain function, instinctive animal aggression, grief-stricken bloodlust, deadly sin, jealousy, the political resentments of right-wing voters, and the moralistic desire for social justice. Barbara Rosenwein has studied the history of angry emotions in depth since the 1990s, and is the author of a recent wide-ranging history of rage, wrath, and revenge from the foundational texts of Buddhism to the present. She concludes that 'anger' is not the name of any single, transhistorical entity.

The Latin word *ira* is one of the ancient terms that is often, and somewhat misleadingly, translated as 'anger' in English. It would better be rendered as 'wrath' or 'vengeance'. One thing the term did share with 'anger', however, was the fact that it could name any of a large family of different states of mind. The Roman philosopher and statesman Seneca noted as much in his treatise on the topic, *De Ira*, in the first century CE. He catalogued bitter, irritable, frenzied ranting, and other forms of ire. Some, Seneca wrote 'simmer down short of shouting', while others were 'savagely physical and not very verbal', and still others tended towards 'complaining and sulking'. 'There are a thousand other varieties', Seneca concluded, 'of this polymorphous evil.'

As ever, one of the big-picture changes revealed by the history of these emotions is a gradual shift from morally to medically inflected ways of thinking about them. Older models saw ire as evil or sinful, while modern 'anger' is more often understood as something physical and explosive, but without any moral judgement necessarily being attached to that. So, Seneca referred to *ira* in all its forms as a 'polymorphous evil', and wrath was one of the 'deadly sins' of Christianity. In more recent decades, though, extreme angry outbursts have been framed instead in psychiatric terms. Freudian psychoanalysis popularized what is often referred to as a 'hydraulic' model, according to which people are full of suppressed rage, which it may be healthier to let out through some relatively safe channel, than to bottle up with the risk of a future explosion. This same metaphor is at play in the diagnosis of 'Intermittent Explosive Disorder', which was included in the *Diagnostic and Statistical Manual of Mental Disorders* (DSM) for the first time in 1980. Popular books by clinical psychologists about managing angry children include Dr Ross W. Greene's 1998 title, *The Explosive Child: A New Approach for Understanding and Parenting Easily Frustrated, Chronically Inflexible Children.* In this picture, people are ticking time bombs rather than moral agents.

Since the late 20th century, we have also learned to diagnose everyday behaviours under headings such as 'Road rage', 'Twitter rage', 'Wi-fi rage', or even 'IKEA rage'—an emotion triggered by the attempt to assemble flat-pack furniture. These modern emotions are a far cry, however, from the concepts of our ancestors from which they are ultimately descended. Returning to the worlds of Greek revenge, monastic curses, jealous homicides, and political protest help us to see our modern, psychological notions of 'anger' from a different perspective, and in their proper proportions.

The pleasures and pains of revenge

The philosopher Martha C. Nussbaum has produced influential studies of emotions, including anger, since the 1990s, in conversation with classical Greek and Roman texts. Hers is a broadly cognitive approach, meaning that she looks for the beliefs and judgements embodied in emotions. This seems especially appropriate for outrage and fury, which can be exceptionally judgemental emotions, based on a fervent belief that I have received some insult or injury, combined with a desire for payback. In her book *Anger and Forgiveness: Resentment, Generosity, Justice* (2016), Nussbaum offers an account of anger along these lines, which connects directly back to the writings of Aristotle about the Greek notion of *orgē* in the fourth century BCE, and through him to a world in which the desire for revenge was a central social concern, as well as a source of pain, bloody violence, and intense pleasure.

Aristotle's recipe for *orgē* had four ingredients: a judgement that I, or a friend, have been injured or insulted; a feeling of pain; an impulse towards revenge; and finally a feeling of pleasure at the thought of how great it will be taking my revenge on the wrongdoer. This final point is worth noting as it marks a difference from most versions of modern 'anger'. In modern psychology, anger is normally considered a 'negative' emotion, whereas for Aristotle, and the ancient Stoics, *orgē* was considered a mixture of pain and pleasure, the latter being found in the sweet thrill of getting one's own back. Aristotle quoted some words of Achilles in the *Iliad*, describing *cholos*—another kind of rage—as being simultaneously bitter, blinding, and choking, like smoke, and yet also 'sweeter than dripping streams of honey'.

Homer's epic, first written down around the 8th century BCE, is sometimes described as a tale about the 'anger' of Achilles, but such an interpretation fails to recognize how distant the *Iliad's* emotional world is from ours. Achilles is driven out of his mind by grief after the killing of his beloved friend Patroclus in battle at the hands of the Trojan prince, Hector. Achilles' loss is expressed initially in wild lamentation and weeping, and then in a frenzied, avenging slaughter of Trojan soldiers. Achilles is described as being 'insane to hack more flesh', and his feelings are conveyed in Greek terms including *menos, thumos,* and *huperthumos,* referring to his spirited energy, ferocity, and 'hyper-fury'. When Hector is finally defeated and begs for his life, Achilles responds,

'Would to god my rage, my fury would drive me now to hack your flesh away and eat you raw—such agonies you have caused me!'

Ancient Greek narratives, including the *Iliad*, which have sometimes been invoked as descriptions of 'anger', tend to offer a window rather on passions and feelings that are simultaneously more painful, more pleasurable, more violent, and more revenge-obsessed than ours. While these thoughts and feelings are far from identical to modern 'anger', they are nonetheless among its ancestors, since western experiences of rage, wrath, and ire have partly evolved through the recovery of Homer, Aristotle, and other classical authors. The shadows of these imposing literary and intellectual figures are cast across later developments.

The connection between personal grief and violent revenge explored in the Iliad has a rich history. From the earliest tragedies in ancient Greece, via the revenge plays of the early modern era, to the romantically blood-soaked operas of the nineteenth century, and the troubled but righteous heroes of action movies in the twentieth, audiences have looked on as the sorrows of one protagonist after another transmute into rage and a lust for revenge, with predictably fatal consequences. In Shakespeare's *Macbeth*, Malcolm urges the grieving Macduff to channel his sorrow towards violence. 'Be this the whetstone of your sword,' Malcolm says. 'Let grief convert to anger. Blunt not the heart, enrage it.'

Although of course it would be a mistake to read Shakespeare as if he were expressing post-Freudian psychological ideas in the 17th century, we can see his naming of impassioned states as 'grief' and 'anger' and connecting them with an archetypal revenge narrative as providing a bridge between the ancient and the modern. Records of witchcraft trials in Shakespeare's time also reveal how words and ideas were evolving. Those accused of witchcraft, who were overwhelmingly female, were accused of being full of 'hatred', 'wrath', and 'anger'. These qualities were evident both in a surly and antisocial demeanour, characterized by the muttering of threats, curses, and profanities, and also in a malicious, underhand campaign of revenge, aided by the devil himself. In such sources, again, we see a sense of 'anger' and related terms which are part way between ancient revenge and modern, emotional anger.

Ancient and modern ancestries come together in another way in the popular 'Angry young man' films of Indian cinema in the 1970s and 1980s. The historian Imke Rajamani has shown how these movies created a new type of male lead, identified by his zeal for revenge. The most notable early example was the performance of Amitabh Bachchan as the police detective Vijay in *Zanjeer* (1973). As a child, Vijay had witnessed the murder of his parents, and the film tells the story of his righteous fight against crime, culminating in finding and killing his parents' murderer (see Figure 11). Films in this genre had a characteristic audio-visual language, with their red-eyed, sweat-bedewed heroes enacting daring, violent exploits against a backdrop of fiery volcanoes, crashing waves, galloping horses, fireworks, gunshots, and dramatic musical scores.

Indian journalists started to describe these films using the English phrase 'angry young man', which had been applied to a group of British playwrights and novelists in the 1950s, and was now imported into the Hindi language. Archetypal narratives of grief and revenge, as in the story of Vijay in *Zanjeer*, were recast in the context of the politics and religion of India, drawing both on ancient Sanskrit images and ideas, and on modern anglophone culture. The 'angry young man' character tended to stand for secular ideals of justice, democracy, and socialism. However, religious imagery was also used, from Sikh, Hindu, Islamic, and Christian sources, reflecting the religious plurality of modern India. Rajamani suggests that Hindu ideas about the fiery gaze and divine anger of the deity Shiva were one inspiration for the angry hero, who sees the truth through his fiercely flaming eyes.

11. This poster for the 1973 movie *Zanjeer* shows the visual imagery of the 'angry young man' role as portrayed here by Amitabh Bachchan.

Whatever the religious imagery of films in the genre, there was no doubt that the vengeful 'angry young man' was on the side of righteousness. Other philosophical and religious traditions, however, have not seen wrath and revenge in nearly such a positive light.

Deadly sins

In the Sermon on the Mount, Jesus advocated forgiveness instead of vengeance, telling his followers to turn the other cheek, love their enemies, and pray for those who persecute them. The letter of St Paul to the Ephesians included the instruction to 'Let all bitterness, and wrath, and anger, and clamour, and evil speaking, be put away from you.' Christian teaching, then, like Buddhism and Stoicism, would seem to be pretty resolutely opposed to angry emotions. It is surprising, therefore, to learn that it was standard practice in European monasteries and convents between the 10th and 13th centuries for monks and nuns to read out long and bitter denunciations of their enemies, cursing them, and asking God and his angels to inflict hideous physical and spiritual punishments upon them. The targets of these curses were often local knights who had illegitimately taken control of buildings, lands, and crops rightfully belonging to the religious community. One such curse ran as follows:

> May the sky above them be made of brass, and the earth they walk on iron. May the Lord toss their bodies as bait to the birds of the sky and the beasts of the land. May their homes be deserted and may no one inhabit them. May the sword devastate them on the outside and fear on the inside. May they be damned with the devil and his angels in hell and may they burn in eternal fires with Dathan and Abiron. Amen. Amen.

So, were medieval Christians against anger or not? To understand better how a prayerful request for divine vengeance against one's enemies could sit alongside the belief that wrath—or *ira*, in Latin—was a deadly sin, we need to set aside modern ideas about people being for or against an 'emotion' called 'anger'.

Ira was one among eight 'bad thoughts' listed by the 4th-century thinker Evagrius of Pontus, who lived as a monk in the Egyptian

12. For European preachers and artists, '*ira*' was a deadly sin involving violence and loss of control, as in this detail of a painting by Hieronymus Bosch from *c*.1500.

desert. This list of impediments that the monks might encounter on their spiritual journey towards God was eventually reduced in number by one to become the seven 'cardinal' or 'deadly' sins. The sin of wrath involved various undesirable elements, including nursing a petty lust for revenge, and behaving in a disorderly, destructive, and violent way. In his painting of the seven deadly sins, made around 1500 CE, the Dutch artist Hieronymus Bosch represented *ira* with a scene showing two men having a drunken brawl outside a tavern, while a woman attempts to keep them apart (Figure 12).

The violent sinfulness of *ira* was also dramatized in a popular medieval poem entitled *Psychomachia*. This was a tale of warfare within the human soul, played out through a series of allegorical battles between personified vices and virtues. In the illustrated versions of the poem that survive from the 9th century onwards,

Ira is a female warrior wielding a sword, and her successful antagonist is the non-violent virtue of *Patientia*—or Patience. The story ends with the defeated *Ira* committing suicide in rage and despair. This image of the self-destructiveness of wrath was also reflected in church architecture of the era, with sculptures showing *Ira* running herself through with a sword, in an agitated state, dishevelled and with her hair standing on end, resembling the devil. While patience was the image of Christ, *ira* was the image of the devil.

So, wrath was sinful when it was ungoverned and disorderly, when it was part of a diabolical pact in witchcraft, and when it involved the illegitimate use of violence. However, if exercised proportionately, by someone with legitimate authority, and in pursuit of worldly or divine justice, wrath could be virtuous. Queens and kings, abbesses and bishops, might have legitimate grounds for *ira*. And, of course, God had the ultimate authority to display wrath towards wrongdoers in exercising divine judgement. Although the libidinous passions of lust and wrath were vicious mental states when allowed free reign, they could become virtuous in the right circumstances, especially when governed by reason. Lust could be used to produce offspring within marriage, while wrath could support the enforcement of justice.

With these ideas in mind, we can see better how a medieval religious community could pray for gruesome retribution on their enemies, while still denouncing wrath as a deadly sin. Formal denunciations, repeated patiently day after day, with the authority of an abbot or abbess, seeking divine approval, were the antithesis of sinful *ira* rather than its embodiment. Instead of taking things into their own hands and seeking violent revenge, the monks and nuns were, with patience, piety, and—we might imagine—only a small amount of glee, calling upon the Almighty to exercise his divine justice in quite specific ways on their troublesome secular neighbours.

According to the Bible, the righteous wrath of God was also connected with God's desire for exclusivity in relation to his chosen people. The 10 commandments begin with two commands not to worship other gods, nor to bow down in front of idols and images, with the accompanying words of warning: 'for I the Lord thy God am a jealous God, visiting the iniquity of the fathers upon the children unto the third and fourth generation of them that hate me'. The words 'jealous' and 'zealous' have a shared root in the ancient Greek *zêlos*, and both convey a fervour, ardent commitment, and fierce protectiveness, which threatens to tip over from devotion to destruction at any moment.

'For jealousy is the rage of a man'

Jealous rage hides in the darker recesses of the ancestry of modern anger, and in the black hearts of those who possessed it. Shakespeare's *Othello*, first performed in 1603, provided the definitive portrayal of jealousy as a deadly 'green-eyed monster'. Othello's wife Desdemona is not guilty of any wrongdoing but Othello is convinced otherwise by his deceitful friend Iago, who whips him up into an unfounded jealous frenzy. In the climactic scene, Othello suffocates Desdemona in her bed, deaf to her pleas, as she protests her innocence and begs for her life. Soon the whole sorry deception is revealed and, having hoped that he might be remembered as an 'honourable murderer', and describing himself as 'one that loved not wisely but too well', Othello kills himself.

The idea that it could be 'honourable' to murder one's wife in this way was implausible in the 17th century, as it is today. The most honourable option open to a gentleman who suspected his wife of having an affair was to demand satisfaction from the other man in an 'honour duel'—with each party appointing a supporter as their 'second' and confronting each other in armed combat at an agreed time and place. This practice started in 15th-century Italy and was adopted by Renaissance gentlemen across Europe. The honour duel arose from hot-blooded, vengeful passions, and yet tried to resolve them through a cold, calculated, and rule-bound ritual. This was comparable to the formalized denunciations of their enemies read out by monks and nuns, channelling what could become sinful wrath into an acceptable and contained form. Duels, however, were increasingly outlawed by modern states during the 18th and 19th centuries, as they sought to establish their monopolies on both violence and punishment.

A second justifiable, although less honourable option for a real-life Othello in the 17th century would have been to kill either his wife or, preferably, the man with whom she had been unfaithful, and then to mount a defence of 'provocation'. Since the middle ages, judicial systems across Europe had found ways to distinguish hot-blooded manslaughter from cold-blooded murder, and to treat the former more leniently. The elegant way that one legal authority made this distinction was that 'manslaughter arises from the sudden heat of the passions, murder from the wickedness of the heart'.

The historian Natalie Zemon Davis has studied official documents known as 'letters of remission', composed in France in the 16th century on behalf of defendants seeking pardons for their crimes. These include tales of men who acted in the sudden heat of their passions, such as a ploughman named Thomas Manny, who successfully sought a pardon in 1530 for stabbing his unfaithful wife to death with a table knife. The letter of remission recorded the 'lewdness and wickedness' of the wife, whom Manny had found in bed with another man. This case was unusual as it was the wife, rather than her lover, who was killed. Wife-killing remained a crime which was much less easily justified or excused than the jealous slaughter of a wife's lover.

In England, the idea that sexual infidelity could constitute a 'provocation' to homicide was confirmed in a definitive judgment in 1671. One John Manning had come home to discover his wife in bed with another man, whom he beat to death with a wooden stool. The question of whether this was to be treated as murder or manslaughter was referred to a higher court, which ruled that it was manslaughter because of the severe provocation. While a man guilty of murder would have been hanged, the reduced punishment for Manning was to be branded on the hand. Further, the court 'directed the executioner to burn him gently, because there could not be greater provocation than this'. In a crucial 1707 judgment setting out this doctrine in more detail, Chief Justice Holt confirmed that, 'if the husband shall stab the adulterer, or knock out his brains, this is bare manslaughter; for jealousy is the rage of a man, and adultery is the highest invasion of property'.

Holt's judgment gave legal expression to social and religious attitudes of the time towards marriage, infidelity, and the passions. His colourful phrase, 'for jealousy is the rage of a man', was a quotation from the Bible, warning against the perils of adultery. It is notable that, for Holt and his contemporaries, a wife was treated as her husband's 'property'. This would remain the case in England until the late 19th century. 'Provocation' in Holt's sense made allowances for the frailties of men when acting under the influence of a rage aroused by offences against their honour, and their property, but within a relatively narrow range. Jealousy and ire were still moral failings, and manslaughter was a serious crime.

The idea that a defence of 'provocation' could be extended to a jealous man who killed his wife, rather than her lover, only came much later and was always controversial. In 1864, the prominent English lawyer James Fitzjames Stephen was involved in the case of a husband who had murdered his estranged wife. The man was found guilty of murder, which Stephen considered the right outcome. To offer any kind of mitigation for a killing on the basis that it was the result of heated passions would have been not only wrong, Stephen thought, but, even worse, un-English. 'It would be deplorable,' Stephen wrote, 'if we came to look upon passion and sentiment as any excuse whatever for crime, after the fashion of Frenchmen and Mexicans.' National stereotypes, along with moral convictions, continued to shape ideas about violent passions and the importance of self-control.

This English attitude persisted into the 20th century, with the example of Othello still a cultural reference point. In resisting a 'provocation' defence in 1946, a Court of Appeal judge stated that, 'Even if Iago's insinuations against Desdemona had been true, Othello's crime was murder and nothing else.' The judge commented further that 'as society advances, it ought to call for a higher measure of self-control in a defendant'. However, the change has in fact been in the opposite direction since then. The 'loss of control' defence introduced in 2009 has a much wider remit than the idea of 'provocation' of which it is the descendant. Today in England or Wales, if a husband is merely told that his wife has been unfaithful, believes it (whether or not it is true), and is enraged to the extent that he loses control and kills her, then he has the chance to ask a jury to reduce his crime to manslaughter. The 'loss of control' defence has been used successfully in exactly this way. In the 21st century, then, unlike any time between the 17th and 20th centuries, a real-life Othello might actually have a chance of being acquitted of murder, on the grounds that he was unable to control his jealous anger.

Natural instincts

Often implicit in the idea that jealous rage is somehow an understandable, albeit a highly regrettable, reaction, are ideas about what level of violent aggression is 'natural', perhaps particularly in men. There seems to be an idea that male self-control is fragile in the face of infidelity and other triggers because of some irresistible, inherited animal instinct. Suggestions about how people carry the deep evolutionary past in the structure of their brains surface in many different contexts, including some quite surprising ones. In 2016, for instance, immediately after the election of Donald Trump as President of the United States, the *Scientific American* blog carried a piece entitled 'Trump's Victory and the Neuroscience of Rage', explaining the result in terms of the operation of the brain's 'threat detection mechanism'. This mechanism can apparently put us in an angry emotional state, ready to 'protect our own tribe, and slaughter another tribe if necessary for our self-preservation'. The speculative idea here was that Trump had been elected because of some invisible, unmeasured 'anger', explained with reference to an even more speculative idea from an imagined evolutionary past—the survival of the fightiest. An innate evolutionary instinct to slaughter our enemies had, apparently, motivated just under half of those voting to choose the more aggressive of the candidates.

This idea that violent rage is somehow 'natural', and embodied, has a long cultural history. Since ancient times, writers have associated rage with the physicality of the human body, with the behaviour of wild animals, and, metaphorically, with other natural phenomena, such as storms and volcanoes. Seneca's irrational and irate man had a flushed red face, quivering lips, grinding teeth, hair standing on end, cracking joints, and a tendency to clap his hands and stamp his feet. Ideas about bodily heat featured in most medieval and early modern medical theories of ire. It was a standard view that in enraged states the blood literally boiled, with all sorts of consequences, including overheating of the heart and, according to at least one 17th-century German medical text, extreme pain in the male genitals.

Certain animals were supposed to be particularly prone to rage, including wolves, bears, tigers, lions, and wasps. The 17th-century man of science Robert Hooke wrote that the bee's sting proved that nature 'did really intend revenge'. One 17th-century visual emblem of choler—the bodily humour associated with ire—showed a young man with a sword standing next to a lion, suggestive of both bravery and cruelty. The English writer Daniel Defoe, in a 1726 book about his former profession as a tradesman, told the story of a shopkeeper who was calm and polite with his customers, but took his daily frustrations out on his family in fits of furious domestic abuse, after which he would sit and weep. Defoe summarized the man's emotional volatility in terms of the creatures he resembled: 'in the shop a soul-less animal that can resent nothing, and in the family a madman; in the shop meek like the lamb, but in the family outrageous like a Libyan lion.'

The most significant moment in the history of the idea that anger is a natural instinct was Charles Darwin's inclusion of human rage alongside the aggressive instincts of bees, dogs, swans, deer, bulls, gorillas, porcupines, and crocodiles in his 1872 book on *The Expression of the Emotions in Man and Animals*. For Darwin, the existence of human expressions such as hair standing on end or the uncovering of the teeth showed that 'man once existed in a much lower and animal-like condition'. Expressions of hatred, rage, and indignation varied widely, Darwin discovered, including going red or purple in the face, or becoming deathly pale, as well as having a rapid or disturbed heartbeat, and displaying some, all, or none of a long list of other behaviours including grinding teeth, quivering nostrils, a foaming mouth, erect hair, or frantic movements. Darwin did not believe there was a single basic emotion called anger, nor that there was a single, universal expression corresponding to angry emotions.

Darwin closely observed the emotional development of his own children, as a source of further evidence. He noted that they took to biting things when 'in a passion', and compared this to the instincts of young crocodiles 'who snap their little jaws as soon as they emerge from the egg'. In the detailed notes he kept about his first child, Darwin recorded that the boy, at the age of 2 years and 3 months, 'became a great adept at throwing books or sticks, &c. at anyone who offended him'. Looking back later in life, Darwin thought that this tendency to angry violence was evident in his sons but not his daughters. So he inscribed the gendered expectations of the upper-middle-class English nursery into humanity's evolutionary ancestry. Such expectations persisted into the 20th century, as parents continued to expect little girls to behave like angels, while allowing boys leeway to express what was now understood as their natural animal aggression.

Over the centuries, white European and North American theorists also looked to science to account for the emotional differences they perceived in people of different origins. These accounts fell into two rough categories—those saying non-European people were too emotional, and those saying they were not emotional enough. These stereotypes existed alongside each other and were sometimes applied simultaneously. Many 'savages', as indigenous people were often called in 18th- and 19th-century texts by European travellers, were supposed to be hysterically prone to childlike bouts of laughter and tears, but also dour, dull, and insensitive.

Ideas about the natural excess or absence of emotions in other races, and the associated belief in a racial hierarchy with white people at the top, were shared across a wide range of moral and political positions. They were held by individuals, such as Darwin himself, who were fiercely opposed to slavery, as well as by its defenders. In the early United States, the moral and political writer Stanley Stanhope Smith argued against the view, put forward by many of his contemporaries, that the non-European races were part of a separate species. Nonetheless, Smith wrote about indigenous American people as an inferior race, who were 'vacant and unexpressive'. The countenance of the indigenous American, Smith said, was generally 'fixed and stupid, with little variety of movement in the features', and this showed that these 'savages of America' knew nothing of the 'finer feelings of the heart' and the 'sentiments of compassion and sympathy'.

Smith's *Essay on the Causes of the Variety of Complexion and Figure in the Human Species* (1787) is one of the texts analysed by the scholar Xine Yao in her literary and cultural history of what she terms 'disaffection' in America. As Yao points out, unfeeling has come in many different forms, each with its own political and moral connotations. The varieties of disaffection include:

> withholding, disregard, growing a thick skin, refusing to care, opacity, numbness, dissociation, inscrutability, frigidity, insensibility, obduracy, flatness, insensitivity, disinterest, coldness, heartlessness, fatigue, desensitization, and emotional unavailability.

From a white perspective in the 18th and 19th centuries, there were certain races whose alleged insensitivity marked them out as emotionally other in a way that revealed inferiority, hostility, or both.

One of the most lasting of these racial stereotypes of unfeeling was the idea of 'oriental inscrutability'. The belief that Chinese people, in particular, displayed a kind of coldness or apathy dates back at least to the 18th century. One Protestant missionary to China in the early 20th century wrote he had been privileged to see the 'hard, emotionless Chinese face as it glowed with the joy that illumines him who knows that Christ is his Saviour'. In 1909, the Anglo-Chinese writer Edith Maude Eton, who used the pen name Sui Sin Far in her writings about the experience of Chinese people in North America, reflected on her experience of this idea:

> I have come from a race on my mother's side which is said to be the most stolid and insensible to feeling of all races, yet I look back over the years and see myself so keenly alive to every shade of sorrow and suffering that it is almost a pain to live.

The perceived inscrutability and insensitivity of non-white people was not in fact a 'natural' racial difference of the kind proposed by post-Enlightenment race scientists. Rather it can be understood, as Yao suggests, as an act of 'affective disobedience' to an abusive emotional regime.

Loaded with information and energy

For those who suffer under abusive structures of power and domination—and their associated structures of feeling—there are several potential strategies of affective disobedience. One could be to seek to escape the maelstrom of passion and suffering altogether in a state of mental tranquillity and detachment. That might have been viable for someone like Seneca, attended by slaves in his villa, pursuing passionless philosophical *apatheia* in the Mediterranean sunshine. It seems a less realistic aim for others. People might instead learn to respond to injustice and suffering with defensive insensibility. The Black feminist poet and essayist Audre Lorde described the apparently hard, protective exterior that women of colour needed to develop. 'In order to withstand the weather,' she wrote, 'we had to become stone.'

Audre Lorde described this state of stony disaffection as a regrettable result of living in a hostile environment, and it was not the only emotional attitude that she analysed. Lorde was also one of the most original and influential writers about anger as a political emotion in the 20th century. In a 1983 essay, 'Eye to Eye: Black Women, Hatred, and Anger', Lorde wrote that every Black woman in America 'lives her life somewhere along a wide curve of ancient and unexpressed angers'. Lorde described her own 'Black woman's anger' as a molten pond, an electric thread, and a 'boiling hot spring likely to erupt at any point, leaping out of my consciousness like a fire on the landscape'. Significantly, Lorde combined these images of heat and eruption with an appreciation of anger as something cognitive—an emotion that revealed a person's beliefs and values. Anger, she said, was 'loaded with information and energy'.

The idea of anger as an effective political energy is widespread in contemporary culture. Over the last 60 years, many have agreed with a version of that idea expressed by the Black rights activist

Malcolm X. During his fight against continuing racial segregation, he described himself as 'the angriest black man in America'. In a speech in the Harlem neighbourhood of New York in 1964, just two months before his assassination, Malcolm contrasted sadness with anger as responses to injustice. 'Usually, when people are sad,' he said, 'they don't do anything. They just cry over their condition. But when they get angry, they bring about a change.' He recommended anger as a raw, but appropriate, emotional response to suffering, and as an emotional attitude which commanded attention and respect, suggesting that the African countries which had achieved independence from colonial rule most quickly were those where people had become angry.

The Freudian idea that depression is 'anger turned inwards' also fed into late 20th-century debates. The radical feminist Andrea Dworkin wrote about this in 1983:

> Depression is commonplace among women because housework is boring, sex is boring, cooking is boring, children are boring, and the woman resents being bored but cannot change it.

Women were expected to find submissive feminine joy in all these frustrating roles, but instead they resulted in a rage which could find no outlet. The housewife's depression 'truly is anger turned inward', Dworkin concluded. Some other women, however, found it frustrating that whatever emotions they felt, they would be told by those who subscribed to this view that 'really', they were angry. The psychologist Carol Tavris, in a popular book on *Anger: The Misunderstood Emotion* (1982), reported overhearing a conversation between two women in a café around this time. The first woman was trying to explain that she was feeling sadness because her father had died, while her Freudian companion insisted this was in fact repressed anger. So insistent was the friend, that eventually the first woman lost her temper, providing yet more evidence for the theory of universal suppressed rage.

The same person can be genuinely detached, resigned, depressed, joyful, grieving, or angry at different moments in their lives, without one of those emotions having to be the 'real' underlying feeling. Emotional diversity is the norm, not the exception. As the philosopher Myisha Cherry puts it in her recent book *The Case for Rage*, 'not all people have the disposition to experience the same emotions in response to the same cause' and this diversity 'makes room for expressions of a variety of fitting emotions in response to a particular cause'. The argument for political rage, then, is not so much that everyone should feel anger, nor feel it all the time, but rather that anger is often one fitting and appropriate emotion among others, including as a response to racial injustice. Anger is a non-ideal emotion responding to a non-ideal society, as Cherry puts it.

The varieties of anger that we debate in the 21st century are distant relations to the frenzied bloodlust of Achilles or the more moderate yet still pleasurable desire for revenge discussed by Aristotle. We can trace the ancestry of our modern angers to half-remembered ideas about sin, violent crime, and the passions, and somewhat more directly to the worlds of psychoanalysis and political protest in the second half of the 20th century. The historical fact that there have been so many different angers, rather than just one, is relevant to ethics and politics. It does not make sense to have one single attitude to all the varieties of rage. Rather than being for or against 'anger' in general, history suggests that we would do well to spell out which version of ire or vexation we are for or against, and why.

Accordingly, a key part of Myisha Cherry's project is to dismantle the complicated, overloaded, unstable structure that has grown up around our term 'anger', and to keep some parts, while jettisoning others. Cherry names the kind of political anger she is interested in 'Lordean rage', to indicate her debt to Audre Lorde's ideas and also to distinguish it from forms of anger in which violent retaliation, hatred, or extermination are the goal. Lordean rage forswears such aims. It is a righteous zeal, full of information and energy. It is a chosen emotional attitude, rather than a 'natural' instinct, and it counts neither vengeance nor violence among its goals. Indeed, we might wonder whether this morally elevated and controlled emotion is a form of anger at all, as most people would understand it. Cherry herself, while certainly seeing Lordean rage as a form of anger, has written that it is also a valuable expression of something else, namely '*agape* love'. And what kind of emotion that might be is another story.

Chapter 6
Looking for love

Given the centrality of Christianity to communal life, learning, and worship throughout large parts of European and American history, it is safe to say that biblical views of love have been among the most widely read and discussed in western history. Of these, one stands out. Composed by the apostle Paul as part of his letter to the fledgling church in Corinth around 55 CE, it is known as the 'Hymn to love'. It begins, 'If I speak in the tongues of mortals and of angels, but do not have love, I am a noisy gong or a clanging cymbal.' 'Love is patient; love is kind,' Paul reminds the fractious Corinthian Christians; 'love is not envious or boastful or arrogant or rude.' Spiritual practices such as prophecies and speaking in tongues will come to an end, Paul writes, but love never ends. 'And now faith, hope, and love abide, these three; and the greatest of these is love.'

The term for 'love' in Paul's letter to the Corinthians was the Greek word *agape*—pronounced a-ga-pay—which took on a special meaning within Christian teaching. It was often translated as *caritas* in Latin and as 'charity' or 'love' in English. The American civil rights leader Martin Luther King used this language of *agape* in a sermon preached in Montgomery, Alabama, in November 1957 on the theme of loving your enemies. King and Rosa Parks had gained national attention two years earlier during the famous Montgomery bus boycott, protesting against racial segregation on public transport. In his sermon on this particular Sunday, King explained that loving your enemies meant resisting the temptation to bring them down and defeat them, even if the opportunity arose. Love, he said was 'creative, understanding goodwill for all men'. Rising to the level of love meant defeating an evil system, while loving the human individuals who 'happen to be caught up in that system'.

King told his congregation there were three Greek terms that could help distinguish between different kinds of love—*eros*, *philia*, and *agape*. *Eros* was a love of beauty discussed by Plato, a yearning of the soul, which had come down to modern culture in the form of a romantic kind of love felt for those we find attractive. Next was *philia*, a love between two friends who do things together, a feeling you have with 'people that you call on the telephone and you go by to have dinner with, and your roommate in college and that type of thing'. *Agape*, finally, was the greatest form of love, an overflowing love that asks nothing in return. In *agape*, King said, you love every man because God loves him, not because he is likeable: 'he might be the worst person you've ever seen'.

King's sermon in Montgomery in 1957 touched on several of the varieties of love which have provided social, cultural, and intellectual historians with endlessly fascinating subject matter, ranging from erotic desire and sexual instincts, to friendship, courtship and marriage, and wider political, ethical, and religious ideals of love. The sermon also touched on a very important point for us, when thinking about love's place in the history of emotions, which is whether love is an emotion at all. King pointed out that Jesus had said, 'Love your enemies', not 'Like your enemies', and commented that love of this kind was not 'sentimental', not about having positive feelings: 'It's not merely an emotional something.' *Agape* love was an attitude, a lasting commitment, a determination to act with understanding and goodwill.

But of course *agape* is a rather special kind of love. Surely even if *agape* does not exactly count as an emotion, familial and romantic love do? Again, the question is undecided. Although studies have shown that 'love' and 'hate' are among the states most readily recognized as good examples of emotions by everyday people, psychologists, it seems, do not think like everyday people—at least not when they are at work. Most lists of 'basic emotions' do not include either 'love' or 'hate'. Several reasons have been suggested for denying that 'love' is an emotion, 'basic' or otherwise. These include the fact that it is a long-lasting state rather than just a fleeting feeling—this is true of all three of King's varieties of love—and also that love necessarily involves another person, and lacks a distinctive facial expression. The prototypical emotion for psychologists is a relatively brief episode in the body and mind of a single individual—such as the flaring up of anger, or a burst of joy—with a distinctive physical state of a kind that can be studied and measured in a laboratory.

The tail of method sometimes seems to be wagging the dog of theory when it comes to the science of love. For instance, in one particularly strident pronouncement in 1984, the leading basic-emotion theorist, Paul Ekman, stated that 'if there is no distinctive universal facial expression associated with a given state, which functions as a signal, I propose that we not call that state an emotion'. Since there is not a facial expression universally recognized as expressing love, then love could not be an emotion. Ekman later softened his view on this point, although he still holds that love is a complex social 'plot', involving more than one person and a range of feelings, and is not an emotion. More recently, some affective scientists have redefined 'love' in a different way, to mean a short burst of warm feeling, a 'micro-moment' of connection. The warm feeling is linked to the 'tend and befriend' hormone, oxytocin, which is also connected with sex and breast-feeding, and so seems to be involved in a range of forms of human bonding and attachment.

Facial expressions and hormonal surges surely accompany some of our emotions some of the time, but for most people such physical accompaniments, even if they are easier to measure in a lab, are not themselves the emotions. The question remains open, then, of whether love is an emotion, and in what sense. For the singer Tina Turner, putting forward a rather jaded view in her 1984 number-one hit 'What's love got to do with it?', love was nothing but a 'second-hand emotion'. Many other possibilities have been suggested, however, including that love is an art, a social practice, a mode of sustained attention, a habit, a drive, a syndrome, a disorder, a way of being in the world, a relationship, a narrative, a commitment, or an ethic. Historians of family, friendship, sympathy, sex, courtship, and marriage have all gone looking for love in the historical record, and have made discoveries which can help us think more deeply about it. Whether love is the highest of religious ideals, the most powerful of human emotions, or not an emotion at all, there is no doubt it is at the heart of the history of emotions, and so is a fitting place to end this introduction to our subject.

From *caritas* to climate change

One of the recurring themes in the history of love is a tension between tidy moral theories and messy emotional realities. No matter how many times I repeat to myself the saintly mantra 'Love is patient, love is kind', I still end up losing my temper with my children. I can console myself that people have always struggled to live up to love's highest ideals. Whether thinking in terms of charity or sympathy, altruism or empathy, the lived experience of families and communities through history has been a compromise between good moral intentions and confounding daily realities. In theory, as St Paul and Martin Luther King both pointed out, Christian love was supposed to be extended to all God's children, even the exceedingly unlikeable ones. In reality, people have found compromises in which their affective resources have been mainly concentrated on a smaller subset of humanity. Charity, as the saying goes, begins at home. And after that you might help your friends.

There is no shortage of evidence to show what wealthy, highly educated, well-connected people thought about love in the past. The opinions and feelings of such people are preserved for posterity in lovingly archived letters and diaries, published tracts and treatises, novels, poems, and plays. It is much harder work to excavate the feelings of less educated ordinary people of modest means. However, the task is not impossible, and social historians have been able to use a range of sources, including legal records, to reconstruct the lives and loves of the 'lower orders'. This is what the historian of family and emotions Katie Barclay has done in her exploration of the history of love in Scotland from around 1660 to 1830, hunting through case records, from both criminal and church courts, for evidence. The result is a portrait of early modern *caritas*, the Latin term for Christian love, and understood both as a moral duty and as a human expression of divine grace.

Barclay understands *caritas* not primarily as an emotion but as an 'emotional ethic'—a framework against which particular feelings and behaviours could be judged. It was an ideal learned from an early age through the catechism of the 'Kirk', the national Church of Scotland. In a series of questions and answers, children and adults alike were taught their duty to love God with 'all our heart, and with all our soul, and with all our strength, and with all our mind', and to 'love our neighbour as ourselves, and to do to others what we would have them to do to us'. The Kirk's confession of faith taught that Christian life was a discipline of 'body, mind, affections, word, and behaviour', and that love of one's neighbour meant 'a full contentment with our own condition and such a charitable frame of the whole soul toward our neighbour, as that all our inwards motions and affections touching him tend unto and further all that good which is his'. Such loving duties were owed by parents to their children, by spouses to each other, and by everyone to their elders and the wider community. Surviving records of thefts, assaults, gossip, slander, fornication, and adultery, which Barclay mines for her evidence, reveal that *caritas* was never an easy ethic to live up to.

So extensive was the remit of *caritas* as an ethical imperative that it was also used as the basis for activities which seem, to modern eyes, less obviously virtuous than being a good neighbour or respecting your elders. This is captured in the title of an article by the church historian Jonathan Riley-Smith—'Crusading as an act of love'—which documents the ways that popes and preachers mobilized a language of fierce, zealous Christian charity in their crusading propaganda. In 1215, Pope Innocent III asked rhetorically how a man could claim to love his neighbour as himself if he learned that 'his Christian brothers in faith and in name are held by the perfidious Muslims in strict confinement', but did nothing to liberate them.

From the 17th century onwards, a 'charity' was also the name for a foundation set up to receive donations and use them in the pursuit of worthy causes. Such organizations proliferated rapidly from the later 18th century, and were closely connected with the culture of sensibility, with its ideal of extravagant compassion. Sensitive and wealthy individuals learned to shed both tears and cash in order to demonstrate their admirable feelings of pity and sympathy for those less fortunate than themselves. The recipients of these charitable feelings and donations included mistreated animals, orphans, 'fallen women', the poor, the injured, the impaired, and the infirm. As the historian and sociologist Bill Hughes has put it, during this period those with disabilities became 'objects of the pathos of the charitable gaze', on the receiving end of patronizing and paternalistic pity, which too often seemed to reinforce rather than reverse social exclusions, while providing wealthy, charitable non-disabled people with a warm moral glow.

Throughout the history of love, people have wondered about the individual's duty to act in order to alleviate the suffering of others, and have found different ways to talk about the feelings involved. Alongside charity, philanthropy, compassion, and pity, a key concept in these debates since the 18th century has been 'sympathy'. In a post-Darwinian world, this term took on a new resonance, as the idea of humanity's shared ancestry with all living things reshaped the moral landscape. Darwin himself had a special interest in love and sympathy, seeing them as social instincts favoured by natural selection. The more loving and sympathetic the members of a group of animals had been, Darwin reasoned, the greater an advantage that group would have had in the struggle for life against less cooperative tribes. He saw evidence of evolved sympathy in pelicans, in baboons, and especially in his beloved dogs, as well as in humans.

The historian of science and emotions, Rob Boddice, has explored the meanings and operations of 'sympathy' within the Darwinian 'moral economy' of the later 19th century. As with Riley-Smith and his exploration of crusading as an 'act of love', Boddice invites readers to suspend their contemporary moral judgements in the interests of historical insight, to try to understand how, for instance, a man of science who performed experiments on live animals could declare himself an animal lover, or how a believer in eugenics could promote state controls on reproduction in the name of virtue and love. There were no simple ways to resolve these moral and emotional tensions, even at the time, and there were vociferous Victorian campaigns against vivisection. The relative values of animal suffering and human health were still far from settled in the post-Darwinian moral economy.

Another commentator on sympathy in Victorian Britain was the novelist George Eliot who, in her 1872 novel *Middlemarch*, speculated that there may be a limit to how much awareness of suffering and tragedy the human frame can take. 'If we had a keen vision and feeling of all ordinary human life,' Eliot wrote, 'it would be like hearing the grass grow and the squirrel's heart beat, and we should die of that roar which lies on the other side of silence.'

Painful as it may be, it is just such a keen awareness of the natural world as Eliot imagined that is at stake in environmental ethics in the 21st century. In her 2021 memoir *Beyond Climate Grief*, the Australian science writer Jonica Newby explores a range of emotional responses to climate change, including worry, anger, denial, courage, grief, and joy, and suggests that one of the most powerful, and her own dominant feeling, is love—love for the fragile natural world and all the beauty within it that is threatened.

A Victorian love story

In 1883, a modern, well-connected young woman called Constance Lloyd wrote to her brother, 'Prepare yourself for an astounding piece of news. I'm engaged to Oscar Wilde and perfectly and insanely happy.' Wilde was already becoming a celebrity, famed for his wit and personality as much as his writing. 'As long as I live you shall be my lover,' Constance told him. They married in London in 1884. 'I feel incomplete without you,' Wilde wrote to his new wife when he had to be away. Soon the couple became parents to two much loved little boys. Cyril was born in 1885, Vyvyan in 1886 (see Figure 13). Later, the boys would recall their father as a 'smiling giant', exquisitely dressed, smelling of cigarette smoke and eau-de-Cologne, making toys for them, and crawling around playfully on the nursery floor. Oscar loved to read stories to his boys, including some he had written himself. He had tears in his eyes when he told them his story of 'The Selfish Giant', explaining to them that 'really beautiful things always made him cry'. Here was the very picture of what historians of the 18th and 19th century have described as the ideal of family life, an emotional, even sentimental, domestic arena filled with parental and familial love, providing the beating heart of a healthy modern society.

Such an idealized 'affective family' was always under threat, though, and for the Wildes, the main threat came when Oscar

13. **Constance Wilde and her and Oscar's first son, Cyril, pictured in 1889, offering an idealized image of familial love.**

started looking for love outside the family home. The infamous and tragic culmination of this part of Wilde's story came in 1895, starting with a libel case foolishly brought by Wilde against the Marquess of Queensberry for accusing him of 'posing as a sodomite', which collapsed, followed by two criminal trials for acts of 'gross indecency' with other men. At the first criminal trial the jury could not reach a verdict, but the government and the prosecution made sure there was no such indecision the second time. Wilde was found guilty and sentenced to two years' imprisonment with hard labour. After his release from prison in May 1897, he immediately left England for a life of exile and disgrace in France and Italy. His health never recovered from his time in prison and he died in Paris in 1900. After his arrest in 1895, despite desperate attempts on his part, Wilde was never allowed to contact or see his sons again. They were told he was dead, even before he was.

During his trials, Wilde was cross-questioned by lawyers about many aspects of his private life, including extravagant love letters he had written to a man we now know to have been his lover, Queensberry's son Lord Alfred Douglas, known to Wilde as 'Bosie'. In one letter, Wilde wrote to Bosie, 'it is a marvel that those red rose-leaf lips of yours should be made no less for the madness of music and song than for the madness of kissing'. Wilde was also grilled about his social encounters with uneducated young men, and about the gifts he lavished on them, including fine clothes, silver-handled walking sticks, and a silver cigarette case. What reason could a man of Wilde's social position and rank have to fraternize with these working-class men who worked as valets or newspaper peddlers, the prosecution wanted to know. Wilde answered that he enjoyed the company of those who were young and carefree, but the jury formed a different impression. These were surely 'renters'—rent boys, whose sexual services Wilde and Douglas had been buying.

The most remarkable moment in Wilde's first criminal trial—one which brought Plato and the philosophy of love into the dock of the Old Bailey, almost certainly for the first time—came when he was asked about a poem written by Alfred Douglas. The poem was called 'Two Loves' and had been published the previous year in a student magazine called *The Chameleon*. It imagined a meeting between two figures, one representing the 'true love' that fills 'the hearts of boy and girl with mutual flame', and the other—a more shadowy figure—who also claims to be called 'love' but, when challenged, concedes, 'I am the love that dare not speak its name.' The lawyer put it to Wilde that these figures stood, respectively, for 'natural love' and 'unnatural love', in other words heterosexual and homosexual love. Wilde denied this vigorously and so the barrister asked, 'What is the love that dare not speak its name?'

Wilde's reply was that the 'love that dare not speak its name' was a beautiful, noble, pure, and spiritual form of affection, of the kind that there was between David and Jonathan in the Bible and 'such as Plato made the very basis of his philosophy'. There was nothing unnatural about it, Wilde insisted:

> It is intellectual, and it repeatedly exists between an elder and a younger man, when the elder man has intellect, and the younger man has all the joy, hope and glamour of life before him. That it should be so the world does not understand. The world mocks at it and sometimes puts one in the pillory for it.

Newspapers reported that this speech was met with 'Loud applause, mingled with some hisses'. It has rightly been remembered as an extraordinary, emotional moment of defiance from a brilliant man facing a cruel punishment for his sexual behaviour. It has an important place in the history of attitudes to homosexuality, as well as in the history of the courtroom as an emotional arena. It also points to a significant Platonic tradition of thinking about love and friendship more broadly.

Wilde's speech conveyed at least a part of the truth about how he understood his love for Bosie and others, although of course the reality was not always as pure, spiritual, and intellectual as he understandably wished to insist it was to the jury at the Old Bailey. Like other young men who studied classics in the 19th century, Wilde learned about ancient Greek ideas of love by studying works including Plato's *Symposium*. There he encountered a range of eye-opening ideas—not only the casual and accepting way in which sex between men was discussed but also the idea, which he would refer to in court in 1895, that one of the highest forms of love was an intellectual friendship between two men. Since the Renaissance, this Platonic form of love had opened up to educated men a form of intense and romantic friendship conceived as a 'marriage of minds'. It allowed for a bond of strong affection between two men of a kind that cannot be easily reduced to today's notions either of a homosexual relationship or of a 'bromance' between straight men. It was an essentially ambiguous form of love, suited to times when such ambiguity could indeed be essential.

The stuff of romance

In the 17th century, writing was described as 'romantic' if it was flowery, overblown, and sensational, in the manner of a medieval 'romance', with its chivalrous knights, daring exploits, and courtly love. When applied to a person, the term meant someone who was a fantasist, struggling to stay in touch with reality. During the 18th and 19th centuries, the 'Romantic' movement in literature added a new layer of meanings, conjuring up images of poets with intense passions, meditating on the beauties of nature, dying dramatic and tragic deaths.

It was also during the 19th century that the idea of pursuing something called 'romantic love' became a widely shared aspiration, and one which has since come to dominate popular understandings of the meaning and nature of 'love'. The rituals of romantic love required time, resources, education, and emotional investment. One needed to be able to read and write, to afford stationery, postage stamps, at least modest gifts for one's beloved, and the leisure time in which to worry about such things. Romantic love became a more widely practised form of courtship as a result of demographic and cultural shifts, including urbanization, state education, the gradual waning of the influence of parents and family on the choice of romantic partners, and the expansion of the middle classes.

Historians tend to agree that modern men and women expected to choose their own spouse, rather than entering into what were in effect arranged marriages, and also that they started to prioritize emotional over material considerations. They wanted to 'fall in love' with the man or woman of their dreams, rather than to marry first, hoping love might follow later. In a wide range of histories of romantic love covering periods from the 18th to the 20th centuries, and several different parts of the world, it seems that these changes towards greater independence from family, and an increased emphasis on emotional fulfilment, were universal trends in the experience of modern love, albeit ones that came to prominence at different times depending on the location. The phrase 'companionate marriage' is often used to refer to the kind of emotional love-match which modern men and women sought, or at least said they sought, as opposed to a marriage of social and economic convenience.

In her study of 18th-century love and courtship, and how it was conducted via letters and gifts, Sally Holloway neatly distils the results of decades of debate among social historians about the balance between utility and romance in modern marriages: 'marriage was neither entirely cold nor universally romantic' and there was no 'clear-cut distinction between strategic unions on the one hand and marriages for love on the other'. Something else that has been relatively consistent across the centuries is the roles both of material culture and of socially prescribed scripts and rituals in what Holloway calls the 'game of love'. In the case of Oscar Wilde, love letters and gifts were crucial pieces of material evidence for a criminal court trying to discern the nature of his relationships with other men. Less romantically, testimony about stained bed sheets was also heard in court. In courtship in the 18th century too, romantic love was expressed, and evidenced, in material stuff. Courting lovers exchanged 'garters, gloves, hair, miniatures, rings, signets, snuffboxes, and valentine cards', as well as love letters, poems, furtive glances, and stolen kisses.

In some cases, a single material object can bear testimony to an extraordinarily complex emotional history, as in the case of an embroidered linen bed sheet, made in the early 18th century, preserved in the textile collections of the British Museum, and studied in minute detail by the historian Sasha Handley. The embroidery work on the sheet was made by Anna Maria Radcliffe, Countess of Derwentwater, and widow of James Radcliffe, executed for his part in the Jacobite uprising of 1715. The embroidered lettering reads, 'The sheet off my dear x dear Lord's Bed in the wretched Tower of London, February 1716'. Microscopic analysis revealed that these words were sewn not in thread but in two different kinds of human hair, which Handley concludes were Anna Maria's own locks, 'intertwined with the gold hair of her recently deceased husband'. An unprepossessing sheet is thus revealed to be a touching material token of the mourning of a political widow, who wished to leave to posterity a relic of her love for her husband. The couple's emotions, like the locks of their hair, were sewn together into the fabric of history.

The symbolism of a bed sheet embroidered with the hair of two married lovers draws attention to the fact that questions of desire, lust, sex, and procreation lay beneath the romantic outer layer of gifts, gloves, and garters. The consequences of an unwanted pregnancy for a woman could be severe and, often, lifelong, in terms of her reputation, social standing, and ability to find a husband, if the father of her child failed to step into that role. Records suggest that about a third of brides were pregnant on their wedding day in Britain, in both the 18th and 19th centuries. Large numbers of children were born outside of marriage too, again with social and emotional consequences. The increasing availability of relatively reliable birth control methods from the late 19th century onwards, and especially the female contraceptive pill from the early 1960s, represented perhaps the single biggest material change to the love lives of women and men in modern history.

Consuming passion

One very simple way to avoid pregnancy had always been available to couples: not to have sex. This was what the clergyman and political economist Reverend Thomas Malthus termed 'moral restraint', and which he advocated in his influential 1798 text, *An Essay on the Principle of Population as it Affects the Future Improvement of Society*. Easier said than done. The resistance of sexual desire to the dictates of reason had been discussed since ancient times. Lust, along with vengeful rage, had always been one of the human appetites of most concern to Christian moralists. Ideas about the irrationality of romantic love have been expressed more recently in a modern, medical way too. The infatuation of the lover has been compared to a psychiatric disorder, characterized as it can be by mood swings, obsessive thoughts, compulsive behaviours, and delusions.

Historically, different cultures and religions have taken a range of attitudes to emotions of sexual desire and erotic pleasure. Ancient Greek sources, as we have seen, reveal that sex between men was deemed healthy and acceptable, at least in some contexts, whether as part of a younger man's development or alongside the intense loving bonds forged between soldiers fighting together. The famous ancient text known as the *Kama Sutra*—a Sanskrit compendium of advice about desire, courtship, sex, and marriage compiled in the 3rd century CE—reflects a Hindu philosophy in which the pleasurable fulfilment of sexual desire is one of the proper aims of life. The text includes advice on many aspects of love and desire, including guidance on different sexual positions. This more open and positive attitude to the sexual side of life is also evident in historical representations of couples enjoying sex in Hindu temples.

In the Christian writings of Augustine of Hippo, in the 4th century, by contrast, the connection between sex and sin is the key concern. 'Concupiscence' was the name Augustine used for a special kind of sickness of the soul, the main symptom of which was a compulsive attraction to material pleasures. One could imagine concupiscence as a relationship to food, alcohol, or recreational drugs, but for Augustine himself the main focus was sex. Before his conversion to Christianity Augustine had been, on his own account in the *Confessions*, obsessed with the idea of physical love. 'To love and to have my love returned was my heart's desire,' he recalled, 'and it would be all the sweeter if I could also enjoy the body of the one who loved me. So I muddied the stream of friendship with the filth of lewdness and clouded its clear waters with hell's black river of lust.' In later life he sought happiness in the love of God rather than in the endless, compulsive quest for ever more sexual pleasure.

The idea that human beings can become consumed by compulsive desires, leading them into a cycle of hope and misery, has also been expressed in the notion of 'cruel optimism' developed in the 21st century by the cultural theorist Lauren Berlant. Both concupiscence and cruel optimism are harmful structures of feeling in which someone is drawn repeatedly to an object of desire, believing it to be a source of fulfilment, when in fact it is an obstacle to their flourishing. Berlant includes fantasies of lifelong, happy, reciprocal romantic love among her examples of cruel optimism. She ponders why people stay attached to these fantasies when 'evidence of their instability, fragility, and dear cost abounds'. In a similar vein, in his 1956 classic on *The Art of Loving*, the psychoanalyst Erich Fromm observed, 'There is hardly any activity, any enterprise, which is started with such tremendous hopes and expectations, and yet, which fails so regularly, as love.'

Fromm had a theory as to what was wrong with modern love. It had become, he thought, not just a consuming passion, but also a consumerist one. 'Our whole culture,' he wrote, 'is based on the appetite for buying, on the idea of a mutually favorable exchange.' And modern love was now based on this idea too. Men and women approached love as they approached shopping. 'Two persons thus fall in love,' Fromm concluded, 'when they feel they have found the best object available on the market, considering the limitations of their own exchange values.' The sociologist Eva Illouz has extended this kind of analysis in depth in a series of works starting with her 1997 book *Consuming the Romantic Utopia: Love and the Cultural Contradictions of Capitalism*. Illouz explores the ways that, since the early 20th century, advertisers used imagery of conventional romantic coupledom to sell a vast array of products, some more clearly linked to romance than others, including 'shampoo, beauty creams, cars, motor oil, and cereals', as well as leisure activities such as cinema-going and holiday-making. Illouz suggests that romantic love replaced religion as the overarching ideological focus in modern culture, and in the 20th century the new utopia was to be attained by buying the right products.

Historians of love can provide evidence which supports this picture of modern love as a consumerist marketplace, in which men and women themselves became both products and consumers. There have been several studies of the use of personal advertisements placed in newspapers, starting in the 19th century, in Europe, America, and beyond, by individuals seeking spouses. Unsurprisingly, these matrimonial adverts aroused suspicion and criticism for bypassing the established conventions of finding a partner through either family or personal connections, and in a way that risked seeming coarse or mercenary. That did not detract from their popularity, however, and they were succeeded both by specialist magazines dedicated exclusively to matrimonial match-making, and also marriage bureaus where clients could apply for expert help. In the 20th century, young people could consume advice columns in newspapers and magazines too. Having spent money on, or borrowed, the publication, they could discover what clothes, accessories, and music they needed to buy in order to maximize their romantic exchange value, as well as the latest vocabulary and ideas to use to show they were up-to-date lovers.

A fascinating example of such an advice column was the 'Dear Dolly' feature in *Drum* magazine, which was founded in South Africa in the 1950s (see Figure 14). The magazine's early success saw it spread into other countries too, including Ghana, Nigeria, and Kenya, and its popular 'Dear Dolly' page has been studied by the historian Kenda Mutongi. Although it was a white-owned publication, most of the writers for *Drum* magazine were black, and it gained a reputation for carrying stories and photographs reflecting everyday African life. The 'Dear Dolly' page printed letters from young men and women asking for advice about relationships. It is difficult to know for sure what proportion of these were genuine, but we do know that 'Dolly' did not exist, except as a photograph of a beautiful female film star at the top of the page. The responses to readers' letters were written by male journalists on *Drum*'s editorial staff. The most common topics in letters sent to 'Dear Dolly' in the 1960s and 1970s were sex before marriage, unwanted pregnancy, and same-sex relationships. 'Dolly' responded with a mixture of flirtation, firmness, and friendship.

The 'Dear Dolly' column continued a trend that had existed since the earliest days of affordable print media in the 19th century, through which men and women could learn the latest languages of love—both verbal and behavioural—through their membership of a virtual, emotional community of readers. This has been true of the often female readerships of romantic fiction through the centuries, who found excitement, escape, and empowerment in stories of love, whether erotic, marital, or occasionally both. We know that some groups of male friends consumed the 'Dear Dolly' column together, reading it aloud, and one can imagine the atmosphere of camaraderie, titillation, and bluster as letters were

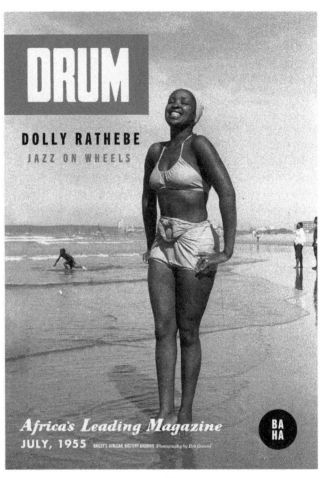

14. Dolly Rathebe, the inspiration of the 'Dear Dolly' advice column, pictured on the cover of *Drum* magazine in 1955.

read out with headlines such as: 'How Can I Learn to Love?' 'Give Me The Secret of a Happy Sex Life!' or 'I Think I'm Gay.' On that final topic, the advice 'Dolly' offered changed across the decades. Whereas readers broaching the topic of homosexuality in the earlier years of the magazine were told it was abnormal and a psychiatric disease, not to mention still criminal in several countries, in 1978 a correspondent worried about being gay was told: 'What you feel is quite natural. Accept your new feelings and do not feel guilty.'

The mess inside

Historians of emotions looking for love have found it in ethical, spiritual, romantic, and sexual forms, in the documentary and material traces left by families, couples, and communities, in bedrooms and courtrooms, in newspapers and novels. Love has existed in many forms, which share powerful feelings of longing and connection. Its history offers an opportunity to reflect on fundamental questions about emotions, past and present. Claire Langhamer, in her history of romantic love in 20th-century England, quotes a famous statement from Karl Marx's 1852 essay 'The Eighteenth Brumaire of Louis Bonaparte':

> Men make their own history, but they do not make it just as they please; they do not make it under circumstances chosen by themselves, but under circumstances directly encountered, given and transmitted from the past.

Similarly, Langhamer suggests, 20th-century lovers made their own romantic histories, but not just as they pleased. They exercised what emotional agency they had within the material and cultural constraints they inherited, as well as new ones such as the idea of 'love at first sight', which allowed people to narrate their love story in a particular way, with agency, they liked to believe, taken away from convention and obligation and given instead to a combination of fate and intense individual emotion.

The quotation from Marx continues with a sentence which could also be applied to historical experiences of emotion: 'The tradition of all the dead generations weighs like a nightmare on the brain of the living.' The idea that our inherited structures of thought and emotion might feel like a nightmare is a useful reminder that emotional lives are full of pain and confusion, as well as love and joy, and that the history of emotions can help us think about that too. Nightmares, dreams, and emotions all offer us a hazy, potent mixture of illusion and reality. To use an image borrowed from the title of the philosopher Peter Goldie's book about emotions, they are *The Mess Inside*. It is a mess on which, as Goldie shows, we can impose a certain amount of order and meaning, using the culturally inherited narratives we tell about ourselves.

The history of emotions shows us not only how the mess inside has been made manifest, both materially and mentally, across the centuries but also how different cultures have construed that very process of manifestation. Curie Virag has written about the Confucian philosopher Xunzi, who developed a theory of feelings and rituals in the 3rd century BCE in China. States of feeling which we might call 'emotions' are, in Xunzi's philosophy, understood as formless, inchoate, and without substance. They do not take on a proper form until they are realized in communal rituals, of the kind used at funerals to mark love and grief for the dead. On this view, the rituals are not an expression of a prior, distinct emotion, but—functioning a bit like an act of observation in quantum physics—they collapse an indeterminate cloud of possibilities into one distinct reality.

Historians of emotions can similarly show how a range of phenomena including grief, rage, love, and joy, which we have learned to think of as vivid inner feelings—the pre-packaged properties of discrete individuals—come into existence in different ways through social performances, communal rituals, and the following of cultural scripts and narratives. It is in those interpersonal and cultural forms that we encounter emotions in their fullest and clearest reality. The most important properties of emotions may not be very emotional at all, if what we mean by 'emotional' is having to do with strong, private, inner feelings. This historical view of emotions tries to move away from certain dichotomies about emotions, according to which they must be either authentic or performed, either fictional or real, either sincere or conventional. They can be all these things at once.

Some scholars have suggested that love is not a basic emotion, or even an emotion at all, for various reasons: because it is too complex, or too long-lasting, because it necessarily involves other people, because it follows a social script, because it is bound up with religious and ethical ideologies, because it comes in endless different forms, because it is so subjective—after all, we don't all love the same people or experience love the same way, because it lacks a distinctive physiology, or a universal facial expression. All those things are indeed true of love. But far from being reasons why love is not an emotion, they are qualities that history has revealed to be the most characteristic and recurring features of those complicated and troublesome, interpersonal and performative, intense, intellectual, and embodied things called emotions.

References and further reading

For each chapter, I have included references to works directly cited, in the order they appear in the text, followed by recommended further reading on the topics of the chapter, arranged alphabetically by author. If a work has already been cited in the references, for the sake of brevity I do not repeat it in the further reading. Readers wanting to find the best starting points for further reading on the whole subject of the history of emotions are directed to the further reading suggestions for Chapter 1.

Chapter 1: The pulse of the past

References

Thomas Carlyle, *The French Revolution: A History*, 3 vols (James Fraser, 1837), chs 1.4.IV and 3.6.I

Jules Michelet, *History of the French Revolution*, trans. C. Cocks (H. G. Bohn,1847), p. 9

Maximilien Robespierre, speech of 26 July 1794, quoted in Irving Babbitt, *Rousseau and Romanticism*, with a new introduction by Claes G. Ryn (Transaction, 1991), p. 136

Lucien Febvre, 'History and Psychology' (1938) and 'Sensibility and History: How to Reconstitute the Emotional Life of the Past' (1941) in Peter Burke (ed.), A *New Kind of History: From the Writings of Febvre*, trans. K. Folca (Routledge and Kegan Paul, 1973), quotations from pp. 9, 12–13, 24

Charles Darwin, *The Expression of the Emotions in Man and Animals* (John Murray, 1872)

Johan Huizinga, *The Waning of the Middle Ages*, available in several modern English translations; first published in 1919

Norbert Elias, *The Civilizing Process,* trans. Edmund Jephcott (Blackwell, 1994), p. 319

Peter N. Stearns and Carol Z. Stearns, 'Emotionology: Clarifying the History of Emotions and Emotional Standards', *The American Historical Review* 90.4 (1985): 813–36

Carol Zisowitz Stearns and Peter N. Stearns, *Anger: The Struggle for Emotional Control in America's History* (University of Chicago Press, 1986)

William Reddy, *The Navigation of Feeling: A Framework for the History of Emotions* (Cambridge University Press, 2001)

Barbara H. Rosenwein, 'Worrying About Emotions in History', *The American Historical Review* 107.3 (2002): 821–45

Jan Plamper, *Geschichte und Gefühl: Grundlagen der Emotionsgeschichte* (Siedler, 2012)

'Sixth Weekly Morale Report', September 1940, Mass Observation Archive. University of Sussex Special Collections

William James, 'What is an Emotion?', *Mind* 9 (1884): 188–205, quotation at p. 194

Audre Lorde in conversation with Claudia Tate in 1982, in Joan Wylie Hall (ed.), *Conversations with Audre Lorde* (University Press of Mississippi, 2004), p. 91

Mary Wollstonecraft, *A Vindication of the Rights of Woman* (1792), chs 2 and 3, at the Online Library of Liberty, <https://oll.libertyfund.org/title/wollstonecraft-a-vindication-of-the-rights-of-woman>

Martha Nussbaum, *Upheavals of Thought: The Intelligence of Emotions* (Cambridge University Press, 2001)

Thomas Cogan, *A Philosophical Treatise on the Passions*, 3rd edn (Cadell and Davies, 1813), p. 245

Further reading

Katie Barclay, Sharon Crozier-De Rosa, and Peter N. Stearns (eds), *Sources for the History of Emotions: A Guide* (Routledge, 2020)

Katie Barclay and Peter N. Stearns (eds), *The Routledge History of Emotions in the Modern World* (Routledge, 2022)

Rob Boddice, *The History of Emotions* (Manchester University Press, 2018)

Rob Boddice, *A History of Feelings* (Reaktion, 2019)

Luke Fernandez and Susan J. Matt, *Bored, Lonely, Angry, Stupid: Changing Feelings about Technology from the Telegraph to Twitter* (Harvard University Press, 2019)

David Lemmings and Ann Brooks (eds), *Emotions and Social Change: Historical and Sociological Perspectives* (Routledge, 2014)

Andrew Lynch and Susan Broomhall (eds), *The Routledge History of Emotions in Europe, 1100–1700* (Routledge, 2020)

Jan Plamper, *The History of Emotions: An Introduction* (Oxford University Press, 2015)

Barbara Rosenwein, *Generations of Feeling: A History of Emotions, 600–1700* (Cambridge University Press, 2015)

Peter N. Stearns and Susan J. Matt (eds), *Doing Emotions History* (University of Illinois Press, 2013)

The Emotions Lab: Feelings Through History, <https://emotionslab.org>

Chapter 2: A map of woe

References

Paul Ekman, 'Basic Emotions', in Tim Dalgleish and Mick J. Power (eds), *Handbook of Cognition and Emotion* (Wiley, 1999), pp. 45–60

William Shakespeare, *Titus Andronicus*, ed. Jonathan Bate (Routledge, 1995), esp. Act 3, Scene 1

C. S. Lewis, *Studies in Words*, 2nd edn (Cambridge University Press, 2013), first published 1960, ch. 3, p. 78

Robert Burton, *The Anatomy of Melancholy*, edited and with an introduction by Holbrook Jackson; and with a new introduction by William H. Gass (New York Review of Books, 2001), pp. 120, 143, 46

Augustine of Hippo, *Confessions*, trans. R. S. Pine-Coffin (Penguin, 1961), book IX.12, p. 202

John Featley, *A Fountaine of Teares, Emptying It Selfe into Three Rivelets, viz. of 1. Compunction, 2. Compassion, 3. Devotion, or: Sobs of Nature Sanctified by Grace* (Crosse, 1646)

Thomas Brown, *Lectures on the Philosophy of the Human Mind*, 4 vols (Tait, 1820), vol. 3, Lecture 52, p. 39

Further reading

Damien Boquet and Piroska Nagy, *Medieval Sensibilities: A History of Emotions in the Middle Ages*, trans. Robert Shaw (Polity, 2018)

Fay Bound Alberti, *Matters of the Heart: History, Medicine, and Emotion* (Oxford University Press, 2014)

Thomas Dixon, *Weeping Britannia: Portrait of a Nation in Tears* (Oxford University Press, 2015)

Elina Gertsman (ed.), *Crying in the Middle Ages: Tears of History* (Routledge, 2012)

Mary Ann Lund, *A User's Guide to Melancholy* (Cambridge University Press, 2021)

Sarah McNamer, *Affective Meditation and the Invention of Medieval Compassion* (University of Pennsylvania Press, 2010)

Marco Menin, *Thinking About Tears: Crying and Weeping in Long-Eighteenth-Century France* (Oxford University Press, 2022)

Kimberley Christine Patton and John Stratton Hawley (eds), *Holy Tears: Weeping in the Religious Imagination* (Princeton University Press, 2005)

Miri Rubin, *Emotion and Devotion: The Meaning of Mary in Medieval Religious Cultures* (Central European University Press, 2009)

Jonathan Sadowsky, *The Empire of Depression: A New History* (Polity, 2021)

Erin Sullivan, *Beyond Melancholy: Sadness and Selfhood in Renaissance England* (Oxford University Press, 2016)

Chapter 3: From passions to emojis

References

Jean Starobinski, 'The Idea of Nostalgia', trans. William S. Kemp, *Diogenes*, 14 (1966): 81–103, p. 82

Susan Matt, *Homesickness: An American History* (Oxford University Press, 2011), p. 92

William Reddy, *The Navigation of Feeling: A Framework for the History of Emotions* (Cambridge University Press, 2001), pp. 96–111, quotation at pp. 102–3

Barbara H. Rosenwein, *Generations of Feeling: A History of Emotions, 600–1700* (Cambridge University Press, 2015), p. 4

Jeremy Bentham, *An Introduction to the Principles of Morals and Legislation* (Clarendon Press, 1996), first published 1789, p. 63

Penelope Gouk and Helen Hills, 'Towards Histories of Emotions', in Penelope Gouk and Helen Hills (eds), *Representing Emotions: New Connections in the History of Art, Music and Medicine* (Routledge, 2005), pp. 15–34, quotation at p. 15

Ruth Leys, *The Ascent of Affect: Genealogy and Critique* (University of Chicago Press, 2017)

James A. Russell, 'Core Affect and the Psychological Construction of Emotion', *Psychological Review* 110.1 (2003): 145–72

Lisa Feldman Barrett, *How Emotions Are Made: The Secret Life of the Brain* (Macmillan, 2017)

Yale Center for Emotional Intelligence, <https://ycei.org/>

Sheldon Pollock (ed.), *A Rasa Reader: Classical Indian Aesthetics* (Columbia University Press, 2016), Preface

Michelle Voss Roberts, *Tastes of the Divine: Hindu and Christian Theologies of Emotion* (Fordham University Press, 2014)

Jean-François Senault, *The Use of Passions*, trans. Henry Earl of Monmouth (Moseley, 1649)

Further reading

Sara Ahmed, *The Cultural Politics of Emotion*, 2nd edn (Edinburgh University Press, 2014)

Karen Bauer, 'Emotion in the Qur'an: An Overview', *Journal of Qur'anic Studies* 19.2 (2017): 1–31

Susan Broomhall (ed.), *Early Modern Emotions: An Introduction* (Routledge, 2017), esp. sections I and II

Thomas Dixon, *From Passions to Emotions: The Creation of a Secular Psychological Category* (Cambridge University Press, 2003)

Thomas Dixon, '"Emotion": The History of a Keyword in Crisis', *Emotion Review* 4.4 (2012): 338–44

Richard Firth-Godbehere, *A Human History of Emotion: How The Way We Feel Built The World We Know* (HarperCollins, 2021)

Ute Frevert, *Emotions in History—Lost and Found* (Central European University Press, 2011)

Ute Frevert et al., *Emotional Lexicons: Continuity and Change in the Vocabulary of Feeling 1700–2000* (Oxford University Press, 2014)

Margaret R. Graver, *Stoicism and Emotion* (University of Chicago Press, 2007)

Monica Greco and Paul Stenner (eds), *Emotions: A Social Science Reader* (Routledge, 2008)

Sianne Ngai, *Ugly Feelings* (Harvard University Press, 2007)

Juanita Feros Ruys, Michael W. Champion, and Kirk Essary (eds), *Before Emotion: The Language of Feeling, 400–1800* (Routledge, 2019)

Bongrae Seok, 'The Emotions in Early Chinese Philosophy', *The Stanford Encyclopedia of Philosophy* (Winter 2021 Edition),

<https://plato.stanford.edu/archives/win2021/entries/emotions-chinese>

Curie Virág, *The Emotions in Early Chinese Philosophy* (Oxford University Press, 2017)

Tiffany Watt Smith, *The Book of Human Emotions: An Encyclopedia of Feeling from Anger to Wanderlust* (Profile, 2016)

Anna Wierzbicka, *Imprisoned in English: The Hazards of English as a Default Language* (Oxford University Press, 2014)

Chapter 4: Terror and the pursuit of happiness

References

Wellbeing data from the UK Government's Office for National Statistics, <https://www.ons.gov.uk/peoplepopulationandcommunity/wellbeing/>

America's Founding Documents at the USA National Archives, including the Declaration of Independence (1776), <https://www.archives.gov/founding-docs>

Benjamin Franklin, 'On True Happiness', *Pennsylvania Gazette*, 20 November 1735, in Jared Sparks (ed.), *The Works of Benjamin Franklin* (Townsend, 1882), vol. 2, pp. 70–2

Edward Rigby, *Dr Rigby's Letters from France &c. in 1789*, ed. Lady Eastlake (Longmans, Green, 1880), p. 62

William Wordsworth, 'The French Revolution, as it Appeared to Enthusiasts at its Commencement' (1804), in Ernest De Selincourt (ed.), *The Poetical Works of William Wordsworth*, vol. 2, online edition (Oxford University Press, 2015)

Helen Maria Williams, *Letters Written in France*, ed. Neil Fraistat and Susan S. Lanser (Broadview Press, 2001), pp. 67–9

Helen Maria Williams, *Letters from France*, 2 vols (Chambers, 1794), vol. 1, p. 181

Monique Scheer, *Enthusiasm: Emotional Practices of Conviction in Modern Germany* (Oxford University Press, 2020), p. 15

Edmund Burke, *A Philosophical Enquiry into the Origin of our Ideas of the Sublime and Beautiful*, 2nd edn (Dodsley, 1759), pp. 58–9, 84–5

Maximilien Robespierre, speech of 5 February 1794, quoted in Peter McPhee, *Robespierre: A Revolutionary Life* (Yale University Press, 2012), pp. 185–6; the speech is available online at the *Liberté,*

Égalité, Fraternité website, <https://revolution.chnm.org/items/show/437>

Timothy Tackett, *The Coming of the Terror in the French Revolution* (Harvard University Press, 2015), p. 346

Nicolas Coeffeteau, *A Table of Humane Passions*, trans. E. Grimeston (Okes, 1621), p. 435

Charles Darwin, *The Expression of the Emotions in Man and Animals* (John Murray, 1872), pp. 239–40

Jan Plamper, 'Fear: Soldiers and Emotion in Early Twentieth-Century Russian Military Psychology', *Slavic Review* 68 (2009): 259–83

Joanna Bourke, 'Fear and Anxiety: Writing about Emotion in Modern History', *History Workshop Journal* 55 (2003): 111–33

Colin Jones, *The Smile Revolution in Eighteenth Century Paris* (Oxford University Press, 2014), pp. 147–9

Germaine Greer, *The Female Eunuch* (McGraw Hill, 1971), p. 10

Mary Wollstonecraft, *A Vindication of the Rights of Woman* (1792), ch. 2, at the Online Library of Liberty, <https://oll.libertyfund.org/title/wollstonecraft-a-vindication-of-the-rights-of-woman>

Nicole Eustace, 'Emotional Pursuits and the American Revolution', *Emotion Review* 12.3 (2020): 146–55

Susan J. Matt, 'Recovering the Invisible: Methods for the Historical Study of the Emotions', in Peter N. Stearns and Susan J. Matt (eds), *Doing Emotions History* (University of Illinois Press, 2013), pp. 42–53, at p. 47

Arlie Russell Hochschild, *The Managed Heart: Commercialization of Human Feeling* (University of California Press, 1983), pp. 3–23

Jamie Bronstein, *The Happiness of the British Working Class* (Stanford University Press, 2023)

Niamh Cullen, *Love, Honour, and Jealousy: An Intimate History of the Italian Economic Miracle* (Oxford University Press, 2019), p. 1

Shulamith Firestone, *The Dialectic of Sex: The Case for Feminist Revolution* (Bantam Books, 1970), p. 90

Further reading

Sara Ahmed, *The Promise of Happiness* (Duke University Press, 2010)

G. J. Barker-Benfield, *The Culture of Sensibility: Sex and Society in Eighteenth-Century Britain* (University of Chicago Press, 1992)

Frank Biess, *German* Angst: *Fear and Democracy in the Federal Republic of Germany* (Oxford University Press, 2020)

Joanna Bourke, *Fear: A Cultural History* (Virago, 2005)

Thomas Dixon, *Weeping Britannia: Portrait of a Nation in Tears* (Oxford University Press, 2015), Part II, 'Enthusiasm', pp. 69–122

Jules Evans, *The Art of Losing Control: A Philosopher's Search for Ecstatic Experience* (Canongate, 2017)

Michael Laffan and Max Weiss (eds), *Facing Fear: The History of an Emotion in Global Perspective* (Princeton University Press, 2014)

Darrin M. McMahon, *The Pursuit of Happiness: A History from the Greeks to the Present* (Allen Lane, 2006)

Jan Plamper and Benjamin Lazier (eds), *Fear: Across the Disciplines* (University of Pittsburgh Press, 2012)

Adam Potkay, *The Story of Joy: From the Bible to Late Romanticism* (Cambridge University Press, 2007)

Monique Scheer, 'Are Emotions a Kind of Practice (And Is That What Makes Them Have a History)? A Bourdieuian Approach to Understanding Emotion', *History and Theory* 51 (2012): 193–220

David M. Turner, 'Disability History and the History of Emotions: Reflections on Eighteenth-Century Britain', *Asclepio. Revista de Historia de la Medicina y de la Ciencia* 68.2 (2016): 1–13

Chapter 5: All the rages

References

Lucius Annaeus Seneca, *Anger, Mercy, Revenge*, trans. Robert A. Kaster and Martha C. Nussbaum (University of Chicago Press, 2010), 18, 1.4.2–3

Barbara H. Rosenwein, *Anger: The Conflicted History of an Emotion* (Yale University Press, 2020), p. 197

Homer, *The Iliad*, ed. Bernard Knox, trans. Robert Fagles (Penguin, 1990), esp. books 18–22

William V. Harris, *Restraining Rage*: *The Ideology of Anger Control in Classical Antiquity* (Harvard University Press, 2001), pp. 55–65

William Shakespeare, *Macbeth*, ed. Sandra Clark and Pamela Mason (Routledge, 2015), 4.3.231–2, p. 269

Imke Rajamani, 'Pictures, Emotions, Conceptual Change: Anger in Popular Hindi Cinema', *Contributions to the History of Concepts* 7.2 (2012): 52–77

Matthew 5:38–48; Ephesians 4:31–2

Lester K. Little, 'Anger in Monastic Curses', in Barbara H. Rosenwein (ed.), *Anger's Past: The Social Uses of an Emotion in the Middle Ages* (Cornell University Press, 1998), pp. 9–35, quotation at p. 10

William Shakespeare, *Othello*, ed. E. A. J. Honigmann (Routledge, 2016), 3.3.168 and 5.2.291, pp. 222 and 331

William Blackstone, *Commentaries on the Laws of England*, 4 vols (Clarendon Press, 1768), vol. 4, ch. xiv, 'Homicide', p. 190

Natalie Zemon Davis, *Fiction in the Archives: Pardon Tales and their Tellers in Sixteenth-Century France* (Stanford University Press, 1987), pp. 1–3

Manning case, Chief Justice Holt, and James Fitzjames Stephen all quoted in K. J. Kesselring, 'No Greater Provocation? Adultery and the Mitigation of Murder in English Law', *Law and History Review*, 34.1 (2016): 199–225, at pp. 208, 214, 221

Viscount Simon's reference to Iago in 1946, quoted in Adrian Howe, '"Red Mist" Homicide: Sexual Infidelity and the English Law of Murder (Glossing Titus Andronicus)', *Legal Studies* 33.3 (2012): 407–30, at p. 422

R. Douglas Fields, 'Trump's Victory and the Neuroscience of Rage', *Scientific American* Blog, 10 November 2016, <https://blogs.scientificamerican.com/mind-guest-blog/trump-s-victory-and-the-neuroscience-of-rage/>

Robert Hooke quoted in Claire Preston, *Bee* (Reaktion, 2006), p. 62

Emblem of 'Choller' in Henry Peacham, *Minerva Britanna* (Dight, 1612), p. 128

Daniel Defoe, *The Complete English Tradesman* (George Ewing, 1726), pp. 75–6

Charles Darwin, *The Expression of the Emotions in Man and Animals* (John Murray, 1872), pp. 12, 243

Charles Darwin, 'A Biographical Sketch of an Infant', *Mind* 2 (1877): 285–94, p. 288

Xine Yao, *Disaffected: The Cultural Politics of Unfeeling in Nineteenth-Century America* (Duke University Press, 2021), pp. 6, 11, 18–19, 171

Norman Kutcher, 'The Skein of Chinese Emotions History', in Peter N. Stearns and Susan J. Matt (eds), *Doing Emotions History* (University of Illinois Press, 2013), pp. 57–73, at p. 57

Audre Lorde, 'The Uses of Anger: Women Responding to Racism' (1981) and 'Eye to Eye: Black Women, Hatred, and Anger' (1982), in *Sister Outsider: Essays and Speeches* (Crossing Press, 1984), quotations at pp. 127, 145, 60

Malcolm X speech, December 1964, in George Breitman (ed.), *Malcolm X Speaks*, 2nd edn (Pathfinder, 1989), p. 107

Andrea Dworkin, *Right-Wing Women: The Politics of Domesticated Females* (Women's Press, 1983), p. 160

Carol Tavris, *Anger: The Misunderstood Emotion*, revised edn (Simon and Schuster, 1989), first published 1982, pp. 38–41

Myisha Cherry, *The Case for Rage: Why Anger Is Essential to Anti-Racist Struggle* (Oxford University Press, 2021), pp. 5, 8, 30–2, 85–91

Myisha Cherry, 'Love, Anger, and Racial Injustice', in Adrienne M. Martin (ed.), *The Routledge Handbook of Love in Philosophy* (Routledge, 2019), pp. 157–68

Further reading

The Sound of Anger, podcast series: <https://emotionslab.org/sound-anger/>

Rob Boddice, *A History of Feelings* (Reaktion, 2019), ch. 1

Jean L. Briggs, *Never in Anger: Portrait of an Eskimo Family* (Harvard University Press, 1970)

Elena Carrera, 'Anger and the Mind–Body Connection in Medieval and Early Modern Medicine', in Elena Carrera (ed.), *Emotions and Health, 1200–1700* (Brill, 2013), pp. 95–146

Thomas Dixon, 'What is the History of Anger a History of?', *Emotions: History, Culture, Society* 4.1 (2020): 1–34

Nicole Eustace, *Passion Is the Gale: Emotion, Power, and the Coming of the American Revolution* (University of North Carolina Press, 2008), pp. 151–78

Gwynne A. Kennedy, *Just Anger: Representing Women's Anger in Early Modern England* (Southern Illinois University Press, 2000)

Charlotte-Rose Millar, *Witchcraft, the Devil, and Emotions in Early Modern England* (Routledge, 2017), esp. ch. 3

Martha C. Nussbaum, *Anger and Forgiveness: Resentment, Generosity, Justice* (Oxford University Press, 2016), esp. ch. 7

Margaret Pernau et al., *Civilizing Emotions: Concepts in Nineteenth-Century Asia and Europe* (Oxford University Press, 2015)

Chapter 6: Looking for love

References

1 Corinthians 13:1–13

Martin Luther King, 'Loving Your Enemies', Sermon Delivered at Dexter Avenue Baptist Church, November 1957, *Martin Luther*

King, Jr. Papers Project, <https://kinginstitute.stanford.edu/king-papers/documents/loving-your-enemies-sermon-delivered-dexter-avenue-baptist-church>

Paul Ekman, 'Expression and the Nature of Emotion', in Klaus R. Scherer and Paul Ekman (eds), *Approaches to Emotion* (Erlbaum, 1984), pp. 319–43, at p. 330

Barbara L. Fredrickson, *Love 2.0: How Our Supreme Emotion Affects Everything We Feel, Think, Do, and Become* (Hudson Street Press, 2013)

Katie Barclay, *Caritas: Neighbourly Love and the Early Modern Self* (Oxford University Press, 2021), pp. 1–5, 35–6

Jonathan Riley-Smith, 'Crusading as an Act of Love', *History* 65 (1980): 177–92, at p. 184

Bill Hughes, 'Invalidating Emotions in the Non-disabled Imaginary: Fear, Pity and Disgust', in Nick Watson and Simo Vehmas (eds), *The Routledge Handbook of Disability Studies*, 2nd edn (Routledge, 2020), pp. 89–101, at p. 93

Rob Boddice, *The Science of Sympathy: Morality, Evolution, and Victorian Civilization* (University of Illinois Press, 2016), ch. 1

George Eliot, *Middlemarch*, ed. Rosemary Ashton (Penguin Classics, 1994), first published 1871–2, ch. 20, p. 194

Jonica Newby, *Beyond Climate Grief: A Journey of Love, Snow, Fire and an Enchanted Beer Can* (NewSouth Books, 2021); cited in Grace Moore, '"This Book Is about How We Feel": Emotions Scholarship, Hope and Climate Activism', *Emotions: History, Culture, Society* 5 (2021): 342–7

Franny Moyle, *Constance: The Tragic and Scandalous Life of Mrs Oscar Wilde* (John Murray, 2011), pp. 72–4, 102

Vyvyan Holland, *Son of Oscar Wilde* (Rupert Hart-Davis, 1954), pp. 52–4, 153, 200

Douglas O. Linder, 'The Trials of Oscar Wilde: An Account', *Famous Trials*, <https://famous-trials.com/wilde/327-home>

Michael S. Foldy, *The Trials of Oscar Wilde: Deviance, Morality, and Late-Victorian Society* (Yale University Press, 1997)

Sally Holloway, *The Game of Love in Georgian England: Courtship, Emotions, and Material Culture* (Oxford University Press, 2019), pp. 4, 9–10

Sasha Handley, 'The Radical History of a Bed Sheet', *History Workshop Online*, 6 June 2017, <https://www.historyworkshop.org.uk/the-radical-history-of-a-bed-sheet/>

Sasha Handley, 'Objects, Emotions and an Early Modern Bed-sheet', *History Workshop Journal* 85 (2018): 169–94

Augustine of Hippo, *Confessions*, trans. R. S. Pine-Coffin (Penguin, 1961), book III.1, p. 55

Lauren Berlant, *Cruel Optimism* (Duke University Press, 2011), pp. 1–3

Erich Fromm, *The Art of Loving* (Harper, 1956), pp. 1–6

Eva Illouz, *Consuming the Romantic Utopia: Love and the Cultural Contradictions of Capitalism* (University of California Press, 1997), p. 37

Kenda Mutongi, '"Dear Dolly's" Advice: Representations of Youth, Courtship, and Sexualities in Africa, 1960–1980', *International Journal of African Historical Studies*, 33.1 (2000): 1–23, at pp. 8, 19

Claire Langhamer, *The English in Love: The Intimate Story of an Emotional Revolution* (Oxford University Press, 2013), p. 19

Peter Goldie, *The Mess Inside: Narrative, Emotion, and the Mind* (Oxford University Press, 2012)

Curie Virág, 'Rituals Create Community by Translating our Love into Action', *Psyche* 28 July 2021, <https://psyche.co/ideas/rituals-create-community-by-translating-our-love-into-action>

Further reading

Katie Barclay and Sally Holloway, 'Interrogating Romantic Love', *Cultural and Social History* 17.3 (2020): 271–7

Alan Bray, *The Friend* (University of Chicago Press, 2003)

Jennifer Cole and Lynn M. Thomas (eds), *Love in Africa* (University of Chicago Press, 2009)

Stephanie Downes, Sally Holloway, and Sarah Randles (eds), *Feeling Things: Objects and Emotions Through History* (Oxford University Press, 2018)

C. Stephen Jaeger, *Ennobling Love: In Search of a Lost Sensibility* (University of Pennsylvania Press, 1999)

Adrienne M. Martin (ed.), *The Routledge Handbook of Love in Philosophy* (Routledge, 2019)

Mark Seymour, *Emotional Arenas: Life, Love, and Death in 1870s Italy* (Oxford University Press, 2020)

Mark Seymour and Sean Brady (eds), *From Sodomy Laws to Same-Sex Marriage: International Perspectives since 1789* (Bloomsbury, 2019)

Phillip R. Shaver, Hillary J. Morgan, and Shelley Wu, 'Is Love a "Basic" Emotion?', *Personal Relationships* 3 (1996): 81–96

Index

For the benefit of digital users, indexed terms that span two pages (e.g., 52–53) may, on occasion, appear on only one of those pages.

Index

Index

THE HISTORY OF LIFE
A Very Short Introduction
Michael J. Benton

There are few stories more remarkable than the evolution of life on earth. This *Very Short Introduction* presents a succinct guide to the key episodes in that story - from the very origins of life four million years ago to the extraordinary diversity of species around the globe today. Beginning with an explanation of the controversies surrounding the birth of life itself, each following chapter tells of a major breakthrough that made new forms of life possible: including sex and multicellularity, hard skeletons, and the move to land. Along the way, we witness the greatest mass extinction, the first forests, the rise of modern ecosystems, and, most recently, conscious humans.

www.oup.com/vsi

Memory
A Very Short Introduction
Michael J. Benton

Why do we remember events from our childhood as if they
happened yesterday, but not what we did last week? Why does
our memory seem to work well sometimes and not others?
What happens when it goes wrong? Can memory be improved
or manipulated, by psychological techniques or even 'brain
implants'? How does memory grow and change as we age?
And what of so-called 'recovered' memories? This book brings
together the latest research in neuroscience and psychology,
and weaves in case-studies, anecdotes, and even literature
and philosophy, to address these and many other important
questions about the science of memory - how it works,
and why we can't live without it.

THE MEANING OF LIFE
A Very Short Introduction
Terry Eagleton

'Philosophers have an infuriating habit of analysing questions rather than answering them', writes Terry Eagleton, who, in these pages, asks the most important question any of us ever ask, and attempts to answer it. So what is the meaning of life? In this witty, spirited, and stimulating inquiry, Eagleton shows how centuries of thinkers - from Shakespeare and Schopenhauer to Marx, Sartre and Beckett - have tackled the question. Refusing to settle for the bland and boring, Eagleton reveals with a mixture of humour and intellectual rigour how the question has become particularly problematic in modern times. Instead of addressing it head-on, we take refuge from the feelings of 'meaninglessness' in our lives by filling them with a multitude of different things: from football and sex, to New Age religions and fundamentalism.

'Light hearted but never flippant.'

The Guardian.

www.oup.com/vsi

RISK
A Very Short Introduction
Baruch Fischhoff & John Kadvany

Risks are everywhere. They come from many sources, including crime, diseases, accidents, terror, climate change, finance, and intimacy. They arise from our own acts and they are imposed on us. In this *Very Short Introduction* Fischhoff and Kadvany draw on both the sciences and humanities to show what all risks have in common. Do we care about losing money, health, reputation, or peace of mind? How much do we care about things happening now or in the future? To ourselves or to others? All risks require thinking hard about what matters to us before we make decisions about them based on past experience, scientific knowledge, and future uncertainties.

CONSCIENCE
A VERY SHORT
INTRODUCTION
Paul Strohm

In the West conscience has been relied upon for two thousand years as a judgement that distinguishes right from wrong. It has effortlessly moved through every period division and timeline between the ancient, medieval, and modern. The Romans identified it, the early Christians appropriated it, and Reformation Protestants and loyal Catholics relied upon its advice and admonition. Today it is embraced with equal conviction by non-religious and religious alike. Considering its deep historical roots and exploring what it has meant to successive generations, Paul Strohm highlights why this particularly European concept deserves its reputation as 'one of the prouder Western contributions to human rights and human dignity throughout the world.

www.oup.com/vsi

THE HISTORY OF MEDICINE

A Very Short Introduction

William Bynum

Against the backdrop of unprecedented concern for the future of health care, this Very Short Introduction surveys the history of medicine from classical times to the present. Focussing on the key turning points in the history of Western medicine, such as the advent of hospitals and the rise of experimental medicine, Bill Bynum offers insights into medicine's past, while at the same time engaging with contemporary issues, discoveries, and controversies.

www.oup.com/vsi

FORENSIC PSYCHOLOGY
A Very Short Introduction
David Canter

Lie detection, offender profiling, jury selection, insanity in
the law, predicting the risk of re-offending, the minds of serial
killers and many other topics that fill news and fiction are all
aspects of the rapidly developing area of scientific psychology
broadly known as Forensic Psychology. *Forensic Psychology:
A Very Short Introduction* discusses all the aspects of psychology
that are relevant to the legal and criminal process as a whole.
It includes explanations of criminal behaviour and criminality,
including the role of mental disorder in crime, and discusses
how forensic psychology contributes to helping investigate
the crime and catching the perpetrators.

www.oup.com/vsi